Only

Believe

Only

Believe

Learning to Walk with God in Trust

Beryl Adamsbaum

Opine
Publishing

Opine Publishing, LLC.
5113 West Running Brook Road
Columbia, Maryland 21044 USA
http://www.opinebooks.com
Email: info@opinebooks.com
Books for Life, Family, and Faith
Opinari (L.) – to think, to reason, to *believe*

Library of Congress Cataloguing-in-Publication:

Adamsbaum, Beryl.
    Only believe : learning to walk with God in trust /
    Beryl Adamsbaum.   p. cm. – (Paths of peace ; 2)
    Includes bibliographical references and index.
    ISBN 097084512X

    1. Trust in God—Christianity. 2. Prayer—
Christianity. 3. God—Knowableness. 4. Christian life.
    I.   Title.

BV4637.A43 2004   248.4
                             QBI33-1200

Cover design by Robert Howard
Printed in the United States of America
DISTRIBUTED TO THE TRADE BY NATIONAL BOOK NETWORK
1-800-462-6420

Contents

About the Author

Beryl Adamsbaum's articles, devotionals, and poetry appear in anthologies and periodicals, including *The Upper Room* and *Grace* magazine. She is a regular contributor to *Day by Day with God*, and is a member of the Association of Christian Writers, England.

Beryl Adamsbaum lives in France, just across the border from Geneva, Switzerland, where she and her husband have been engaged in Christian ministry for over thirty years with people from many countries. Formerly a language teacher, she is involved in writing, teaching, translating, speaking, and counseling.

"Be not afraid, only believe."
Mark 5:36
King James Version

Preface

O *nly Believe* is the second book of my trilogy
on prayer. In *Seeking God's Face*, the first
book in this series, I referred to various prayers
in the Bible. I shared my confidence that prayer
is a tremendous privilege, not a mechanical exercise or duty. I related how my relationship with
God deepened as I learned to take him at his
word, trust him, and count on his promises.

Now, through this second book, we will delve
more deeply into the reasons and motivations
behind prayers in the Bible. I have carefully chosen specific prayers for us to focus on together.
We will learn to trust God more as we understand the circumstances that prompted these
prayers and take special note of the way they are
expressed.

In these prayers, there is much we can learn
and benefit from. Our praying will be transformed as we enter more fully into God's purposes in these ways.

The Bible tells us that "without faith it is impossible to please God, because anyone who
comes to him must believe that he exists and
that he rewards those who earnestly seek him"

(Heb. 11:6). Do you believe that he exists? Do you believe that he rewards those who earnestly seek him? Then act upon that belief. Come to him, seek him earnestly.

Our relationship with God is built on faith and trust. In Psalm 62:8, King David exhorts his people to trust God "at all times." We are to trust him not only when all is going well, but also through the difficulties and uncertainties of life.

Do you remember the promise God gave to Solomon after the dedication of the temple? We need to take God at his word, believe him and trust him. If we, who are his people, will humble ourselves, pray, seek his face, turn from our wicked ways, repent of our sin, and turn to God (see 2 Chron. 7:14), then we have the assurance that he will hear us, forgive us, and bring us whatever form of blessing, restoration, and satisfaction is appropriate.

Jesus encouraged people to have faith in him, to trust him, to believe in him. Remember Jairus, the synagogue ruler who came to ask Jesus to heal his daughter? Jesus was delayed and the girl died, yet Jesus told the father, "Be not afraid, only believe" (Mark 5:36-King James Version). Then Jesus raised her from the dead. *Only believe.*

1

Fog

Those of us who live in or near Geneva, Switzerland, spend part of each winter under a blanket of dank, murky, damp fog. Outside of the relatively small "Geneva basin," other people enjoy clear skies and warm sunshine. The word "basin" explains it all: bad weather is funneled to the Geneva end of the lake—Lac Léman or Lake Geneva—and just hangs there.

But the lake is not the only physical feature in the immediate area. Geneva is also surrounded by mountains: the Jura to the west, the Alps to the southeast; and two smaller ranges, the Salève and the Voirons, across the border in France—all of which are made equally invisible by fog.

Faith

On those foggy days, who in their wildest imaginings could ever envision the breathtaking sight of the Mont Blanc, culminating at 4,800 meters, its snowy white peak etched against an intense blue sky? The fog completely obliterates all such beauty and majesty. However, that does not change the fact that up there, with the sun shining all around, the Mont Blanc rises in all its superb splendor! We know it is there; we believe it is, even though we cannot see it from down below.

Most of us who live in the area have been able, at one time or another, to drive the few kilometers needed in order to leave the cold, dark, clammy fog behind and enter a world of light and warmth. And what a contrast it is! We feel we can really breathe again as we drink deeply of the fresh, clean air. We experience warmth as we lift our faces to the caressing rays of the sun. Our stiff, heavy limbs are invigorated as we step out freely and joyfully in the brightness.

It is like living in two different worlds: the disagreeable opaqueness "down here" and the luminous transparency "up there." Doesn't that remind you of the spiritual reality of "now we see through a glass, darkly; but then face to face" (1 Cor. 13:12-KJV)? Our lives on this earth are often clouded by fear, pain, sorrow, or uncertainty. At times, we cannot perceive the love of God. We are blind to spiritual truths. We do not know which way to turn. All seems dark. However, in spite of the dimness and fog, God's promises remain true. We must hold onto them. *Only believe.* After all, if we could see clearly at all times, who would ever need to exercise faith? "Faith is being...certain of what we do not see," the writer of the letter to the Hebrews tells us (Heb. 11:1).

God-fearing Job

Job is a good example of someone who did not understand what was happening to him. If anyone was in a complete metaphorical fog, it was Job. But he continued to trust God in spite of devastation, bereavement, illness, and well-meaning friends who only added to his distress.

At the beginning, we see this man as one who lived an upright life. Riches, prestige, reputation—he had everything going for him and acknowledged the source of his prosperity: "He feared God and shunned evil" and was known to be "the greatest man among all the people of the east" (Job 1:1;3). Job was richly blessed.

However, Job was soon up against the harsh realities of life, facing extreme tests and trials. God brought him to Satan's notice, saying, "Have you considered my servant Job? There is no one on earth like him, he is blameless and upright, a man who fears God and shuns evil" (Job 1:8).

We can't help wondering why God drew attention to Job that way. If God had kept silent about Job, perhaps none of the terrible tragedies would have befallen him. Job might have continued living his easy, prosperous, God-fearing life.

Testing

Job could have spent all his days in the sunshine, with no sign of fog! Would he have been better off in the long run? Did God have a reason for allowing Satan to test him? We know that God's purposes are always pure and just. We know they result in our ultimate good, even when our sight is dim and we do not understand, even when we cannot see beyond the fog. That is where faith comes in. *Only believe.*

Satan's challenge is, of course, that it is not for nothing that Job fears God. "Have you not put a hedge around him and his household and everything he has? You have blessed the work of his hands, so that his flocks and herds are spread throughout the land. But stretch out your hand and strike everything he has, and he will surely curse you to your face," suggests Satan (Job 1:10-11).

God takes up the challenge and tells Satan that he may touch everything Job has, but he may not lay a finger on Job. As Satan takes advantage of God's permission to test Job, notice who has set the limits, notice who is really in control.

Very soon, Job finds himself bereft of children, servants, flocks, and herds. All his wealth and possessions have gone. In his grief, he does an amazing thing. "He fell to the ground in worship" (Job 1:20). He is in no doubt of God's sovereignty. "The LORD gave and the LORD has taken away," he says (Job 1:21). The text says that, "Job did not sin by charging God with wrongdoing" (Job 1:22).

But Satan has not finished with his evil schemes. He comes back before the Lord who points out to Satan that Job "still maintains his integrity" (Job 2:3). Satan is then allowed to test him further, but still within limits: he may touch Job, but he may not take his life (see Job 2:6). In spite of everything that happened, Job's faith in God never wavers, and he affirms with assurance, "When he has tested me, I will come forth as gold" (Job 23:10). *Only believe.*

Greater worth than gold

The apostle Peter picks up this theme of gold, explaining to his readers, "Now for a little while you may have had to suffer grief in all kinds of trials. These have come so that your faith—of greater worth than gold, which perishes even though refined by fire—may be proved genuine and may result in praise, glory and honor when Jesus Christ is revealed" (1 Pet. 1:6,7). Peter explains that God allows trials in order to test the reality, the genuineness of our faith. Just as gold is refined by fire, so our faith is tested and purified by the trials that we go through, and ends up even more precious than fine gold.

Peter does not make light of the trials we go through. He is not minimizing the pain. Compared with eternity, what could amount to a lifetime of suffering is described as being only "for a little while." Similarly, the apostle Paul says, "our light and momentary troubles are achieving for us an eternal glory that far outweighs them all" (2 Cor. 4:17).

Into the sunshine

The book of Job ends on a triumphant note as the Lord brings him through the fog and into the sunshine, leading him into a relationship of greater trust. We read that, "The Lord blessed the latter part of Job's life more than the first" (Job 42:12). Let us, too, learn to trust God in the darkest times and remember that "in all things God works for the good of those who love him, who have been called according to his purpose" (Rom. 8:28).

Even though difficulties and trials may come your way and you do not understand—you do not *see*—what is going on, you are already enjoying eternal life if you have entered into a relationship with God through Jesus Christ. Even in the midst of grief, you can experience the joy of sins forgiven and the assurance of spending eternity with your heavenly Father, in whose "presence is fullness of joy" (Psalm 16:11–KJV).

The next time the fog comes down, literally or figuratively, remember that there is sunlight and warmth beyond the grayness. And, in spite of the present reality, "Let us fix our eyes on Jesus" (Heb.12:2), our Savior, the One who is "the light of the world" (John 9:5) and "the bright Morning Star" (Rev. 22:16).

2

Deserving or Not?

Luke 7: 1-10

As we reflect on trusting God in the dark times, the healing of the centurion's servant recorded by Luke is worthy of note. This account is one of two occasions in the Bible where we read that Jesus "was amazed" (Luke 7:9). Why this amazement?

Humility of a great man

In chapter seven of Luke's gospel, we are introduced to a centurion who lives in Capernaum. He was obviously a greatly respected man, one who was used to having people follow his orders. When one of his valued servants became sick to the point of death, this Gentile centurion sent Jewish leaders to ask Jesus to come and heal his servant.

These "elders of the Jews" obviously thought very highly of the Roman officer, because they "pleaded earnestly" with Jesus on his behalf. They gave good reasons why Jesus ought to answer his prayer and respond to his request for help. After all, the centurion loved the Jewish nation, and he had built their synagogue. In their estimation, he was *worthy* of Jesus' help. "This man deserves to have you do this," they said (Luke 7:4). The centurion, however, had a far different opinion of himself.

Jesus was already on his way. He was not far from the centurion's home when the officer did an interesting thing. He sent word to Jesus not to come to his house after all, because he did not consider himself worthy to receive Jesus. He "sent friends to say to him: 'Lord, don't trouble yourself, for I do not deserve to have you come under my roof'" (Luke 7:6).

Why did he send his friends? Why did he not go himself? He said: "I did not even consider myself worthy to come to you" (Luke 7:7). What humility on the part of this man who was accustomed to having people under him, who was used to giving orders and commands and being obeyed! He recognized his own unworthiness.

Power in the word

But what of the poor servant who was dying? The centurion was so convinced of Jesus' power and authority that he knew he could heal his servant even from a distance. "Say the word, and my servant will be healed," he said (Luke 7:7b).

"Say the word." Jesus had only to speak for the servant to be healed. The power was in the word he spoke. That is when we read that Jesus "was amazed." He was amazed at this lucid and humble man's faith. "I have not found such great faith even in Israel," said Jesus to the crowd that was following him (Luke 7:9).

At the conclusion of this account, we read that the servant was found well when the men, who had been sent to Jesus, returned to the house. Jesus had healed in response to the centurion's faith. *Only believe.*

Saving faith

Author Leon Morris wonders about the nature of the centurion's faith. Certainly, the centurion believed that Jesus could and would heal his servant. Did his faith reach beyond that healing? Did he, in fact, go so far as to believe in Jesus and accept him as his Lord and trust him for salvation?

Let us be clear that our salvation is not based on any merit of our own. Like this Roman officer, we need to recognize our own unworthiness. We do not in any way *deserve* God's grace. It is by faith that we are saved. And faith means relying fully on the finished work of Christ at Calvary. *Only believe.*

Abram believed the LORD, and he credited it to him as righteousness.

Genesis 15:6

3

Pleading with God

Genesis 18:23-33

O ne of the most precious of all human relationships is friendship. We can relax and
be ourselves with our friends. We enjoy spending
time with friends who share our interests or
hobbies. We learn to trust, depend on, and sup-
port one another. True friends open up their
hearts and share deeply.

God's friend

What a tremendous privilege to be called God's
friend! One person we read of in the Old Testament who earnestly sought God and was re-
warded by being called "God's friend" (James
2:23) is Abraham. Abraham is commended because of his faith. Moreover, his faith was not
only intellectual belief. It was essentially practi-
cal. His faith was put to the test and proved real
because he acted upon it. James tells us that

Abraham's "faith and his actions were working together, and his faith was made complete by what he did" (James 2:22). Faith, to be real, has to be exercised.

In the book of Genesis, we find Abraham pleading with God, not for himself, but for the wicked city of Sodom. The intimacy of his relationship with God is such that he dares to come before him in boldness and beg for mercy for the town. The one who is called "God's friend" engages in dialogue with the Almighty and even dares to challenge him: "Will you sweep away the righteous with the wicked?" (Gen. 18:23). Is he questioning God's justice? Regardless, God pursues the question and answer session, and graciously agrees to spare the town if there are "fifty righteous people" (Gen. 18:24) in it.

Realizing that there probably weren't fifty righteous people in Sodom after all, Abraham humbly asks God if he will spare the city for the sake of forty-five righteous people. Once again, God agrees. Abraham keeps bargaining with God until they get down to ten: "Then he said, 'May the Lord not be angry, but let me speak just once more. What if only ten can be found there?' He answered, 'For the sake of ten, I will not destroy it'" (Gen. 18:32).

Of course, there were not even ten righteous people in the city of Sodom, and God did have to destroy it. The point is, however, that Abraham, "God's friend," felt free to plead with God. His relationship with God was such that he came pretty close to pestering him. God wants his children to have this freedom.

Test of faith

The test of Abraham's faith that James refers to is recorded for us in Genesis 22. God had given to Abraham and his wife Sarah in their old age a son from whom they had been told would come "a great nation" (Gen. 12:2). Now God tells Abraham to sacrifice Isaac, his only son.

Nothing in the Bible record tells us anything about the struggle that such a command must have inevitably produced within Abraham. Neither does the Bible tell us how Sarah reacted. Isaac himself seems puzzled (Gen. 22:7), as he wonders where the "lamb" for the burnt offering is, but we do not read of him rebelling in any way when his father, Abraham, binds him and places him on the altar he had built.

The biblical account gives us just the bare facts. Without demur, Abraham obeys and trusts. It is only as he picks up "the knife to slay his son" that an angel stays his hand and remarks, "Now I know that you fear God, because you have not withheld from me your son, your only son" (Gen. 22:12). We read that "Abraham looked up and there in a thicket he saw a ram caught by its horns. He went over and took the ram and sacrificed it as a burnt offering instead of his son" (Gen. 22:13). What remarkable faith! Abraham was prepared to obey God without question.

"I have called you friends"

Are you "God's friend"? Jesus says to his followers, "You are my friends if you do what I command...I have called you friends, for everything that I learned from my Father I have made known to you" (John 15:14,15). His command is that we love each other in the same way that he loves us.

If you are sure of his love for you and if you reflect this love in your relationships with your fellow Christians, then avail yourself of the privilege that is yours. Come into his presence at any time and in any place to plead and intercede as Abraham did! "Come boldly unto the throne of grace" (Heb. 4:16-KJV).

But you may say, "I don't have as much faith as Abraham." It is not the amount of faith you have that counts but where that faith is placed. Put your faith in almighty God. Jesus said, "If you have faith as small as a mustard seed, you can say to this mountain, 'Move from here to there' and it will move. Nothing will be impossible for you" (Matt. 17:20). *Only believe.*

4

Be Explicit!

Genesis 24:1-67

*A*braham's servant is praying next to a well outside a town in Mesopotamia. With him are ten of his master's camels laden with goods. Why is he there? He has been sent by Abraham to find a wife for his son, Isaac. How is he to know which girl to choose? Well, that is precisely what he is praying about!

Here is the substance of his unambiguous prayer: "O LORD, God of my master Abraham, give me success today, and show kindness to my master Abraham. See, I am standing beside this spring, and the daughters of the townspeople are coming out to draw water. May it be that when I say to a girl, 'Please let down your jar that I may have a drink,' and she says, 'Drink, and I'll water your camels too'—let her be the one you have chosen for your servant Isaac. By this I will know that you have shown kindness to my master" (Gen. 24:12–14).

And what happened? God heard and quickly answered this servant's prayer! In fact, "before he had finished praying, Rebekah came out with her jar on her shoulder....The girl was very beautiful, a virgin; no man had ever lain with her" (Genesis. 24:15a; 16a). *Only believe.*

Who was Rebekah? Interestingly enough, she just happened to be a relative of Abraham! She was Abraham's brother Nahor's granddaughter (see Gen. 24:15b). You see, Abraham did not want Isaac to marry a girl from Canaan where he was living. That is why he had sent his servant to his own country and his own relatives to find a wife for Isaac.

Specific requests

Abraham's servant's prayer was detailed and precise. That is what draws us to this prayer—its explicitness! We who can so easily be unclear in our thinking and "woolly" in our praying should follow this example. Instead of just asking God to bless so and so, we should bring before him the specific needs and situation of the person for whom we are praying.

Yes, God knows the circumstances of the people we pray about so much better than we do. But he wants us to intercede according to their needs.

God's answer

Let us look at the specifics of how the Lord answered the prayer of Abraham's servant. We read that Rebekah "went down to the spring, filled her jar and came up again. The servant hurried to meet her and said, 'Please give me a little water from your jar.'

"'Drink, my lord,' she said, and quickly lowered the jar to her hands and gave him a drink" (Gen.24:16–18). She would have been carrying the jar on her head, which explains why she had to lower it. So far, the details correspond to the way the servant had phrased his prayer. Let us see what happens next. We read: "After she had given him a drink, she said, 'I'll draw water for your camels too'" (Gen. 24:19). She went ahead and did this, and all the time the servant was observing her, to see if she really was the answer to his prayer! *Only believe.*

When the camels had finished drinking, the servant gave Rebekah a gold nose ring and two gold bracelets. He asked her about herself and her family and enquired as to whether her father could give him a room for the night. Learning that she was related to Abraham, the servant bowed down and worshiped God (see Gen. 24:26). He knew he was close to journey's end and that his trip had been successful. He thanked God for answering his prayer: "Praise be to the LORD, the God of my master Abraham, who has not abandoned his kindness and faithfulness to my master. As for me, the LORD has led me on the journey to the house of my master's relatives" (Gen. 24:27).

Rebekah ran to the house to tell her family what had happened. Her brother Laban hurried down to the spring to fetch the servant, brought him up to the house, offered him hospitality, and provided straw and fodder for the camels. The servant would not eat until he had revealed the reason for his journey. He explained why Abraham had sent him, how he had prayed at the well, and how God had answered his prayer.

Both Laban and Bethuel, Rebekah's father, were convinced that this was from God. In their certainty, they quite abruptly told the servant to take Rebekah and go, so that she might become the wife of his master's son, according to the Lord's will. The servant's reaction was to give presents of clothes and jewelry to Rebekah and other expensive gifts to her family, including her mother (see Gen. 24:50,51,53).

Happy ending

The next morning, as the servant was impatient to leave, Rebekah's mother and brother requested that he allow Rebekah to wait ten days before going. But Rebekah decided that she and her maids would leave immediately, with Abraham's servant and his men.

A lovely ending accompanies this story. We read that Isaac "went out to the field one evening to meditate, and as he looked up, he saw camels approaching. Rebekah also looked up and saw Isaac. She got down from her camel and asked the servant, 'Who is that man in the field coming to meet us?'" (Gen. 24:63–65a). When Rebekah learned that the man was Isaac, "she took her veil and covered herself"; and soon, Isaac "married Rebekah. So she became his wife, and he loved her" (verses 66, 67).

Opportunity knocks!

I prayed very specific prayers when I felt chal-
lenged to reach out to the people in our apartment building, people I hardly ever saw! I began
to pray specifically that God would bring me into
contact with them. I was amazed at the way he
answered my prayer and the speed with which
things happened.

First, Claudia from across the way asked my
husband and me to look after her cat while she
and her husband were on vacation. Next, Natha-
lie and Roger, two floors up, dropped their nut-
crackers over their balcony. They landed in our
yard, giving me a pretext to go up and return
them! Then while out walking one day, I found
myself in step with a neighbor from the next
building, which enabled us to chat together. After welcoming the new neighbors right next door,
we had them over one evening to get to know
them. Soon after, we were invited to their home
to partake of their eight-year-old daughter's
birthday cake!

The most amusing answer to my prayer concerns Catherine who lives immediately above us.
One day I suddenly noticed water dripping
through our ceiling. Catherine's apartment had a
leak! We sent for a plumber, and then the man
from the insurance company came to check the
damage. Catherine and my husband and I had to
fill in forms for the insurance company. It was a
lovely opportunity to spend time with her. We
made an evening of it and invited her to dinner.

I had made a specific prayer request and received a very rapid, comprehensive answer! Of

course, my husband and I need to feed these relationships, and as we do so, I continue to pray for opportunities of reaching our neighbors with the gospel. *Only believe.*

5

Wrestling with God

Genesis 32:1-32

Have you ever wrestled with God? I can remember crying out to God one sleepless
night for the salvation of one of my sons. I had
prayed for such a long time, for many years, and
yet could see so little of God's working in his life.

That night I was filled with despair. Why
wasn't God doing anything? I struggled within
myself and wept. I kept on pouring out my soul
to the Lord. Did I doubt his ability to save? No, of
course not. Then why didn't he act in this par-
ticular situation?

Little by little, I began to feel the Lord was
rebuking me for my lack of faith. *Only believe*
were the words that came to me. If Jesus raised
Jairus' daughter from the dead, then he can still
give spiritual life and light to those who are walking in darkness.

God's hidden ways

After wrestling with God during that night, I ended up saying to him, as did a father who brought his son to Jesus for healing, "I do believe; help me overcome my unbelief" (Mark 9:24). Who am I to say that God is not doing anything anyway? He works in hidden, mysterious ways that we cannot perceive. He is sovereign. He is all-powerful. "Surely the arm of the Lord is not too short to save, nor his ear too dull to hear," proclaims the prophet Isaiah (Isa. 59:1).

If you are wrestling with God over some issue and doubting his ability or willingness to meet you in your need, then listen to the words of Jesus and act upon them: *Only believe.*

Did you know that there is one person in the Bible who was said always to be wrestling in prayer? What a ministry Epaphras had! The apostle Paul wrote to the Christians in Colosse about him: "He is always wrestling in prayer for you, that you may stand firm in all the will of God, mature and fully assured....he is working hard for you..." (Col. 4:12,13).

I wonder if we really think of prayer as "work." Some years ago, my husband and I had the pleasure of receiving into our home Ajith Fernando, Director of Youth for Christ in Sri Lanka. He was in the area to speak at a seminar organized by a group of churches in France and Switzerland. Some time later, when reading his book, *The Jesus Driven Ministry*, I was struck by his statement that prayer is "the most important work" he has done in over twenty-five years of ministry, I think Epaphras would have agreed with him!

Important decision

Why does most of my "wrestling" take place at night, I wonder, especially as sleepless nights are very much an exception to the rule for me! Another sleepless night comes to mind, however, from the time when our church was praying that God would provide a new pastor.

That morning, a Sunday, the pastoral search committee's remaining candidate had preached in our church. His wife and one of his daughters were also there. Afterwards, during a fellowship meal, he shared a bit about himself and his family, and answered some questions. As a church, we had an important decision to make: we needed to know whether this man was the one that God had chosen to be our new pastor.

It was an emotional time for me. My husband had been pastor in that church since it began— we had been serving there for over thirty-two years. And now that it was time for us to retire, we wanted to be sure that the appointed successor was God's choice.

I lay awake that night, thinking over all that had been done and said during the service that morning. I agonized over the choice the church had to make. I could only plead with the Lord to keep us from making a mistake. I prayed that, as a church, we might know God's mind on the matter and that he would lead us to make the right decision. Then I had to just hand things over to the Lord and trust that he would answer my prayer. *Only believe.*

Reminder of God's promise

Genesis 32 records a full night of wrestling in prayer by a man called Jacob. At the time, Jacob was very afraid and distressed. He had learned that his brother Esau was coming to meet him. Jacob had decided to divide all his people, flocks, and herds into two groups. That way, if Esau stole in and attacked one group, the other group might escape.

Then, after thanking God for all that he had given to him over the years, Jacob confessed to God his fear that Esau would come and attack him and his family. He asked God to keep them safe. Jacob then concluded his prayer reminding God of his promise to Jacob's grandfather Abraham, that he would make him and his descendants "like the sand of the sea, which cannot be counted" (Gen. 32:12). Why do you think Jacob reminded God of this? I think it was another way of expressing his trust in God.

After all, if God's promise was to be fulfilled, there was no way that Esau could kill him off! What he is saying in effect is that Esau might want to attack him, but as God had promised to greatly multiply Jacob's descendants (as Esau had sold his birthright to Jacob—see Gen. 25:29-34), God's promise to Abraham would be fulfilled through Jacob. So Esau would not be able to follow through on his intent. Therefore, Jacob believed that God would answer his prayer and save him.

Blessed

Jacob stayed there all night after sending his servants ahead with gifts for Esau. Having settled his wives, maidservants and eleven sons on the opposite side of a stream, Jacob also sent across "all his possessions" (Gen. 32:23).

> So Jacob was left alone, and a man wrestled with him till daybreak. When the man saw that he could not overpower him, he touched the socket of Jacob's hip so that his hip was wrenched as he wrestled with the man. Then the man said, "Let me go, for it is daybreak."
>
> But Jacob replied, "I will not let you go unless you bless me."
>
> The man asked him, "What is your name?"
>
> "Jacob," he answered.
>
> Then the man said, "Your name will no longer be Jacob, but Israel, because you have struggled with God and with men and have overcome."
>
> Jacob said, "Please tell me your name." But he replied, "Why do you ask my name?" Then he blessed him there.
>
> So Jacob called the place Peniel, saying, "It is because I saw God face to face, and yet my life was spared" (Gen. 32:24-30).

A note in my Bible says "Israel means *he struggles with God*," and "Peniel means *face of God*."

Transformation and trust

What are we to make of this strange wrestling match, which took place throughout a night until sunrise?

Up until then, Jacob had relied a lot upon his own ingenuity for his elaborate plans with regard to Esau. Did he also think he could claim the land that God had promised to Abraham's descendants by his own strength, cleverness, and guile?

The result of the wrestling match was a transformed Jacob. His challenger, by wrenching his hip, took away his strength. Thereby, Jacob realized that it was only by trust in God's promise that he would obtain the land and not by any devious means or by his own power.

At this time, Jacob's name was changed from Jacob, which means *deceiver*, to Israel, because *he had struggled with God*. The wrestling match brought him through to real trust in the Lord.

What about you? Have you ever wrestled with God? If so, what was the outcome? Maybe you are struggling right now with some issue. Maybe you are facing some difficult problem. Maybe you think you'll overcome in your own strength. God wants you to yield to him. "'Not by might nor by power, but by my Spirit,' says the LORD Almighty" (Zech. 4:6). *Only believe*. Trust God as Jacob finally did and discover what W.H. Griffith Thomas calls "the secret of all real spiritual power and blessing."

6

Not Convinced?

Exodus 3:4-4:17; Jeremiah 1:6-9

I can look back at times in my life when I felt really incapable of doing what I knew I had to do. I remember, as a young teacher, being confronted with my first class of students. I was terrified of them, but God took away my fear and enabled me to get on with the job.

There have been many occasions over the years when I have catered for relatively large numbers of people in our home, and even found myself enjoying doing it too—and I am not a particularly good cook!

I would not normally choose to speak in public. Each time, I feel like saying, "Help! I can't!" Even as I walk up to the front of a hall to begin speaking, I ask for God's enabling and equipping. And each time he meets me in my need.

Carmen, a nurse in our church, served the Lord as a missionary in Guinea Conakry and the Congo. Years later, she received a call to work among leprosy patients in Mozambique. This required learning Portuguese and adapting all over again to a different country's customs and culture.

Did Carmen say to God, "Who am I that I should learn a new language at my age and leave all that is familiar for a foreign land?" If she did, we were not aware of it, although agreeing to go was not an easy step for her to take. She went in obedience to God's call, knowing that he would be with her and equip her.

Not me!

Let's consider two of God's key men in the Old Testament, Moses and Jeremiah, and see how they responded to God's call.

The people of God were living under oppression in Egypt, and God was concerned for them. He heard their cries for help and planned a way of rescue. From a burning bush in Midian, he revealed himself to Moses, who was tending the flocks of his father-in-law Jethro.

We know that "Moses hid his face, because he was afraid to look at God" (Ex. 3:6). God had chosen Moses, of all people, to deliver the Israelites.

"Go," said God to Moses, "I am sending you to Pharaoh to bring my people the Israelites out of Egypt" (Ex. 3:10). Immediately Moses responded, "Who am I, that I should go to Pharaoh and bring the Israelites out of Egypt?" (Ex. 3:11).

This is a very human reaction. "Who am I?" Basically, Moses was saying, "I can't do it." Have you ever felt that way? God calls you to do something that you know is beyond your natural capacities and capabilities. How do you respond? Are you convinced?

When God calls

Moses had an ongoing debate with God. Didn't he know he could count on God's presence and equipping? When God calls, he always enables and equips. He had promised Moses, "I will be with you" (Ex. 2:12). Shouldn't that have been sufficient? Yet, when God gave signs to convince him that he would succeed in his mission, Moses was still recalcitrant.

We should be encouraged, however, because we are often just like that ourselves! We are very conscious of our shortcomings, and we are afraid to move out of our comfort zone. Likewise, Moses was aware of his own weakness and felt unable. But God was patient with him. At one time, Moses said, "O Lord, please send someone else to do it" (Ex. 4:13). God became angry with him, yet he acceded to Moses' request by sending his brother Aaron to do the talking.

Even though God directed Moses and Aaron in their confrontations with Pharaoh, all did not go smoothly, and the promised deliverance was long in coming. In fact, things got worse at first, as Pharaoh reacted by making conditions even more difficult for the Israelites.

Moses and Aaron could easily have given up hope. Moses was obviously very discouraged. He said: "O Lord, why have you brought trouble upon this people? Is this why you sent me? Ever since I went to Pharaoh to speak in your name, he has brought trouble upon this people, and you have not rescued your people at all" (Ex. 5:22,23).

Remember, "the LORD would speak to Moses face to face, as a man speaks with his friend" (Ex. 33:11). And, we know that Pharaoh finally did let the people go! Under Moses' leadership, with God's equipping, they journeyed out of Egypt and through the wilderness. Later, Moses still needed confirmation from God: "You have been telling me, 'Lead these people,' but you have not let me know whom you will send with me" (Ex. 33:12).

What a wonderfully reassuring answer God gave him: "My Presence will go with you, and I will give you rest" (Ex. 33:14). Who else does Moses need if God is with him? What more would be needed to convince him that he could do what God was asking of him?

In the same way, God promises to be with us. "Never will I leave you; never will I forsake you" (Heb. 13:5). As with Moses and Abraham (called "God's friend"), this intimacy with God is available to us in Jesus Christ. Let us draw near to him, count on his presence with us, and experience the rest and peace he wants to give us. What more do we need to be convinced?

Like Moses, Jeremiah had a very difficult mission, prophesying to God's disobedient, idolatrous people. It is not easy to persevere when problems come our way and we face opposition.

Jeremiah had a reaction similar to Moses when God called him to be a prophet. Jeremiah wrote: "'Ah, Sovereign LORD,' I said, 'I do not know how to speak; I am only a child'" (Jer. 1:6).

But God answered him in a very affirming way, assuring him of his presence and telling him not to be afraid. Then God touched his mouth and said, "Now, I have put my words in your mouth" (Jer. 1:9).

God has given one of the most beautiful promises of the Bible through the mouth of his prophet Jeremiah:

> 'For I know the plans I have for you,' declares the LORD, 'plans to prosper you and not to harm you, plans to give you hope and a future. Then you will call upon me and come and pray to me, and I will listen to you. You will seek me and find me when you seek me with all your heart. I will be found by you,' declares the LORD (Jer. 29:11-14).

Do we begin to doubt God's leading and wonder whether he will answer our prayers? Surely, he has much to teach us through the lives of Moses and Jeremiah, among others. And he teaches us through our struggles, as he taught them. We must not lose heart and begin to despair. Even though we are weak, God promises us his strength. "My power is made perfect in weakness," he says (2 Cor. 12:9). Are we convinced? If we are, then let's prove it by acting on his promises. *Only believe.*

Is any one of you in trouble? He should pray. Is anyone happy? Let him sing songs of praise.

James 5:13

7

Joy and Trials

James 5:13

O nce upon a time a beautiful blond girl flew across the miles to a foreign land. There, kind people welcomed her. As time went on, she grew in grace and comeliness, and opened up her heart to the love of God. At the same time, in the far-off land of Denmark, a young prince rose into the air, only to land in the same city as the girl. Endowed with rich intelligence, our Danish prince, well read and bright, discovered too the love of God and gave his life to him. One day Prince Charming met his princess and swept her off her feet. They were married and lived happily ever after.

That is how I began the sermon at the wedding of a young couple in our church, describing how they had first met and how their relationship had developed. That introduction was spoken, if not exactly in jest, then at least with tongue in cheek! I went on to say that we are not living in a fairytale world, but in the real world of which sin and evil are a part and where nothing is perfect.

Happiness and joy

The bride had asked me to preach on Psalm 37, which refers to wicked men who act selfishly according to their own desires and for their own ends. In contrast, we are exhorted to "trust in the LORD and do good; dwell in the land and enjoy safe pasture" (Psalm 37:3). "If you trust him," I said to the happy couple, "God will take care of you, give you security and meet your needs." *Only believe.*

"Radiant joy" was the theme of the message at another wedding we attended. Many of us were gathered to share in the happiness and joy of the young French couple. "Is anyone happy? Let him sing songs of praise," writes James (5:13b). And we did! We sang enthusiastically. We sang joyfully. We sang sincerely. We sang songs of praise to God for his goodness.

Later, we continued the joyful celebration with a wonderful spread of refreshments served in glorious sunshine in a beautiful wooded area on the banks of Lake Geneva.

Pain and anguish

A short time after that wedding, we heard about another engaged young couple that, in joyful anticipation, had been preparing their own marriage ceremony. However, their wedding would never take place, for we heard the news that a road accident had cost them both their lives. Imagine the shock and the anguish of their families and friends.

Why? Why did God allow such a thing to happen? At such times, we struggle to understand and to trust God.

It would perhaps be presumptuous to try to find an explanation for the tragedy. We could say much about sin, evil, God's goodness, love, and sovereignty—and about human responsibility; we could say much about heaven where "there will be no more death or mourning or crying or pain" (Rev. 21:4). However, there are many things we do not understand. Often we are obliged to say quite simply, "I don't know."

As I have been writing this chapter, news has come of the murders of three Christian missionary doctors at a hospital in Yemen. Again, we ask how this can be. We can give multiple examples of tragic accidents, terrorist attacks, senseless violence, and brutal murders.

Conflicting emotions

How do you handle the two conflicting emotions—joy and pain? How can I rejoice in my good fortune when my brother or sister is sorrowing or grieving? Is it possible to cut ourselves off from suffering in the world, shut ourselves up in our ivory tower, and enjoy all that life has to offer, when next door or on the other side of the world people lack the basic necessities of life?

And what about inconsistency within ourselves? The apostle Paul, who called himself "the worst of sinners" (1 Tim. 1:16), must have grieved deeply over his own sin.

Prayer and praise

We must learn to live with this ambivalence, this paradox, this contradiction of grief and joy. For if *joy* is a theme running throughout the whole of Scripture, so is that of *suffering and pain*. And what does the apostle James exhort such a person to do? "Is any one of you in trouble? He should pray," is his advice (James 5:13). James also says, "Consider it pure joy, my brothers, whenever you face trials of many kinds" (James 1:2).

The apostle Peter says something similar: "You greatly rejoice, though...you may have had to suffer grief in all kinds of trials" (1 Pet. 1:6). How can this be? These statements seem completely incompatible and contradictory.

God's attributes

How is it possible for us to "greatly rejoice" and "suffer grief" at the same time? I think the answer to that question is found in God himself. Let me explain. As Christians, we profess to believe in the one true God as revealed to us in Jesus Christ through the Scriptures.

Who is this God in whom we trust? It is important that we understand God's character. God's attributes have to be balanced one against the other in order for us to see him as he really is so that we do not end up with a distorted picture.

For example, if we talk about God's justice without mentioning his love and mercy and compassion, we could be left with a picture of a harsh, unbending, unloving Judge. If we emphasize his love at the expense of his justice, he becomes weak and condoning.

One aspect of God's character, which is always a source of great encouragement and comfort to me, is his sovereignty. He is in charge, as it were. He is in control. We must never forget that this sovereign God is a God who loves us and wants the best for us.

Temptation or testing?

So when trials come upon us, we can always say, "If God has allowed this, there is a reason for it, a good reason."

However, how do we know whether suffering and trials are sent from God to test us or from the devil to tempt us? Testing from God should result in strength and maturity. Tempting from the devil, if yielded to, would result in defeat and destruction, which are his aims and desires.

It can be confusing to realize that one word in the Greek translates to both "test" and "tempt" in our English Bibles! Trials that come into our lives can be looked upon as either tests from God or temptations from the devil. However, can bad things be used of God for our ultimate good? Sometimes we are genuinely perplexed as we wonder whether difficulties that come our way originate from our heavenly Father or from the one who is known as "the father of lies" (John 8:44).

Scripture shows us the glorious fact that God can transform any situation, good or bad, to bring good out of evil. The very things that the devil would use to destroy us can be used by God to build us up, strengthen, and equip us.

Paul's experience

In this trilogy's first book, *Seeking God's Face*, I referred to a testing experience of the apostle Paul. Paul wrote: "To keep me from being conceited...there was given me a thorn in my flesh" (2 Cor. 12:7). So far, so good. God gave him this "thorn in the flesh," whatever it was, presumably for a good reason, to keep him from becoming conceited.

The problem arises when we read further and see that this thorn in the flesh was, in Paul's words, "a messenger of Satan, to torment me" (2 Cor. 12:7). Who sent it? God or Satan? Was it to stop Paul from being conceited or was it to torment him? I think that nowhere more clearly do we see that both God and the devil are at work— God for good and Satan for evil, in the life of the believer.

That is not much comfort if we are thinking in terms of dualism, a heresy that says that good and evil are two equal forces competing against each other. Remember, God is sovereign, supreme. The devil is powerful—we must not underestimate his power—but God is all-powerful. Jesus rose victorious over sin, death, and the devil. God's purposes can never be thwarted. All that Satan purposes for evil, God can turn around and transform into good.

God's grace

You may be familiar with the name of Joni Eareckson Tada. At age seventeen, Joni dove into the Chesapeake Bay, Maryland, and hit her head. Her neck broke, and she ended up a quadriplegic. Joni believes that Satan schemed that she would break her neck, hoping to ruin her life. But God used her handicap, she says, to answer her prayer for a closer walk with him. Joni glorifies God from her wheelchair.

The supreme example of this understanding of suffering is the crucifixion of Jesus. When "Satan entered into" Judas (John 13:27), the result was his betrayal of his Lord. "Wicked men" (Acts 2:23) put Jesus to death. We can only conclude that these men were instruments of the devil. Yet, all this was done "by God's set purpose and foreknowledge" (Acts 2:23). Who, then, was ultimately in control? God was, of course. God transformed that evil deed perpetrated by the devil into a manifestation of his redemptive love and grace, offering salvation to all humanity.

Only believe.

I can do everything through him who gives me strength.

Philippians 4:13

8

Heard

1 Samuel 1:1-20

I n the previous chapter, we focused on James 5:13: "Is any one of you in trouble? He should pray." Now we consider a person in the Old Testament who was troubled and who did pour out her heart and soul before God in prayer. She was Hannah, who was "down-hearted" and "in bitterness of soul," who "wept much" (1 Sam. 1:8,10).

Characteristics of sadness

Let's see the contrast between the characteristics of sadness manifested by Hannah and the marks of happiness exhibited by the joyful wedding guests mentioned in the last chapter: the wedding parties felt happiness and joy, expressed through singing and music; sadness takes refuge in prayer. Celebratory joy bursts into song; suffering breaks into tears. Eating and drinking are part of a happy wedding reception; Hannah "would not eat" (1 Sam. 1:7).

Privilege of prayer

Hannah "prayed to the Lord" (1 Sam. 1:10). What a privilege in moments of anguish or ongoing suffering to share everything with God. The Lord loves us so much that he died for us. He who "took up our infirmities and carried our sorrows" (Isa. 53:4) wants to be intricately involved in all that befalls his children. He identifies with us.

On one of the family's annual visits to the temple in Shiloh, Hannah poured out her heart to God. She expressed all her sadness, anguish, grief, and pain. In her misery, she "kept on praying to the LORD" (1 Sam. 1:12). It was a long silent prayer. "Hannah was praying in her heart, and her lips were moving but her voice was not heard" (1 Sam. 1:13). It was between her and God, this intimate, deep communion.

Eli, the temple priest, observing the intensity of her soundless supplication, assumed that she was drunk! Hannah quickly explained: "I am a woman who is deeply troubled. I have not been drinking wine or beer; I was pouring out my soul to the LORD....I have been praying here out of my great anguish and grief" (1 Sam. 1:15,16). She cast her burden on the Lord, just as the apostle Peter exhorts us to do: "Cast all your anxiety on him because he cares for you" (1 Pet. 5:7).

Transformed countenance

What did Hannah do next? Having finished pray-
ing, she quite simply "went her way." She "ate
something." Her countenance was transformed:
"Her face was no longer downcast" (1 Sam. 1:18).
Because her prayer had been answered? No.
There is no mention of an answer at this point.
She doesn't yet know how God will answer her
prayer. *Only believe.*

Do you remember the definition of faith given
in the letter to the Hebrews? "Faith is *being sure*
of what we hope for and *certain* of what we do
not see" (Heb. 11:1, emphasis added). Hannah
had faith. She knew that she could leave her
burden with God. She cast all her anxiety on
him, knowing that he would take care of her.
But, nothing in her situation had changed—yet.

Cause of distress

And what was Hannah's situation? She was
childless. In addition, because of her barren
state, her husband's other wife, Peninnah, who
had children, was always subjecting her to much
unkindness and provocation. After her fervent
prayer, Hannah remained childless, and Peninnah was just as unkind to her. Yes, the situation
remained the same. But Hannah had changed!
She, who wept, wept no more. She, who would
not eat, partook of food. She, who was "down-
hearted" and "in bitterness of soul," had a peace-
ful expression on her face.

Dealing with problems

What do you do when you are deeply troubled? Not everyone deals with serious problems in the way that Hannah did. We can go into denial, pretend problems do not exist, and refuse to acknowledge them. Such a reaction would only harm us, both physically and psychologically. And the difficulties would still be there.

We could try to forget our problems by immersing ourselves frantically in all kinds of activities. Or, we could take to drink or drugs, sinking deeper into depression as what initially seemed to be gloriously liberating becomes an enslaving nightmare.

On a trip to Western Australia, I visited Fremantle Prison. I wondered what the British convicts there must have thought when, between 1850 and 1860, they built the pale limestone walls that were to become their own jail. As I looked at the cells and the gallows where 43 men and one woman were hanged between 1888 and 1964, I began reflecting that many people today are unwittingly constructing a prison for themselves. People become slaves to drink, drugs, sex, money, power, and other things—in efforts to solve problems—and are unable to break their chains, as the desired "solutions" imprison them.

However, what they cannot do in their own strength, Jesus can do for them. "I can do everything through him who gives me strength," exclaimed the apostle Paul (Phil.4:13). The Bible tells us in fact that we are all slaves to sin, and as such, we deserve to die. "The wages of sin is death" (Rom. 6:23). But Jesus died in our place, so that we might live. "You have been set free from sin" (Rom. 6:18).

Another way to try to deal with our problems can be to seek a kindred spirit, someone to open up to and share all that is on our heart. If that person were caring enough, then such a step could be a great encouragement. However, some problems we may find difficult to share. In any case, our friend or counselor may not be in a position to help much.

Blessed assurance

Remember what Hannah did. She prayed, and what a difference that made to her. What relief! What blessed assurance, even before she saw the answer! What peace and calm flooded her soul! "God is our refuge and strength, an ever-present help in trouble" (Psalm 46:1). Hannah experienced what the psalmist experienced. What about you?

The biblical account continues: "In the course of time, Hannah conceived and gave birth to a son" (1 Sam. 1:20). God answered Hannah's prayer beyond the immediate peace that she received. He gave Hannah a child!

You have made known to me the path of life....

Psalm 16:11

9

Why Pray – and How?

1 Samuel 1:1-20 (continued)

"*I*s any one of you in trouble? He should pray" (James 5:13). Why pray? To give a satisfactory answer, we need to know to whom we pray. When we *are* in trouble, there is no one better to turn to than our heavenly Father, who knows us through and through, who understands us completely, who loves us, who is perfectly aware of our circumstances, and who is all-powerful to help us. Let it be clear that we don't *only* pray when we are "in trouble." But when we are in trouble, we should pray!

God's love for you

Hannah, of the previous chapter, prayed to the "LORD Almighty" or the "LORD of hosts" (1 Sam. 1:11-Revised Standard Version). In the French equivalent of the Good News Bible, Hannah is said to have prayed to the "God of Israel." We know that God had chosen the people of Israel for one reason alone. Was it because they were better or stronger than the other peoples of the world? No, "the LORD did not set his affection on you and choose you because you were more numerous than other peoples, for you were the fewest of all peoples. But it was because the LORD loved you..." (Deut. 7:7,8).

God had chosen them because of his love for his children! When Hannah prayed she knew she was addressing the God who loved her. What about us? We know, even better than Hannah, how much God loves us. The apostle Paul writes to the Romans that "God demonstrates his own love for us in this: While we were still sinners Christ died for us" (Rom. 5:8). Never doubt God's love. He proved his love for you by dying in your place. Jesus says, "Greater love has no one than this, that he lay down his life for his friends" (John 15:13).

God's sovereignty and power

What does the expression "the LORD Almighty," used by Hannah, teach us about God? It tells us something of his power and sovereignty. When we pray to him, we know that he is able. He "is able to do exceeding abundantly above all that we ask or think," writes Paul to the Christians in Ephesus (Eph. 3:20–KJV).

What do we learn from the title "the LORD of hosts"? It is interesting to note that it is used for the first time in the whole Bible in 1 Samuel 1:3, where we read that Hannah's husband, Elkanah, "used to go up year by year from his city to worship and to sacrifice to the LORD of hosts at Shiloh" (RSV). Hannah picked up on this expression in her prayer (1 Sam. 1:11-New International revised Version)! The "hosts" are the heavenly armies standing ready to obey the orders of the Lord. Once again, this title speaks to us of the Lord's sovereignty and omnipotence.

Hannah addressed herself to this sovereign God who can do all things and who loved her. She submitted to him, knowing that his way was best. She left with God her worries, her trouble, and her distress. She trusted that he does all things well. Do you have this same vision of almighty God? Come to him, whatever your problem might be. Confide in him. Cast your cares on him. Because he is all-powerful and he loves you. *Only believe.*

How should we pray?

Having asked *why* we should pray, *how* should we pray? Hannah can help us with this problem too. There are several lessons we can learn from her prayer.

First, as already mentioned, Hannah knew and trusted the God she was addressing. This left her free to get right to the point: "Please see how I'm suffering! Show concern for me! Don't forget about me! Please give me a son!" (1 Sam. 1:11–NIrV).

She opened herself up completely to God. She poured out her heart and soul to him. "See how I'm suffering!" *See!* She did not hide how she was feeling. She shared her deep pain with God. She cried, "Show concern for me!" or "Have mercy on me."

We come across this little phrase elsewhere in the Bible. For example: David prayed, "Be merciful to me" (Psalm 4:1). In the New Testament, two blind men followed Jesus, shouting, "Have mercy on us" (Matt. 9:27). In addition, we so often read that God heard this cry for help and showed concern for his children and had mercy on them.

Then Hannah asked God to remember her and to give her her heart's desire. There was no beating about the bush. Her request was simple, clear, explicit, and precise: "Please give me a son!" You can pray in the same direct way. You can open yourself up to God and pour out your distress. You can trust him and ask him to have mercy on you; you can plead with him to give you what you need or desire.

We noted earlier that Hannah prayed for a long time: "She kept on praying to the Lord" (1 Sam. 1:12). I wonder what she was saying all that time? The text does not tell us exactly, but Hannah herself gives us an indication. When she replied to Eli's mistaken accusation that she was drunk, she explained that she was "deeply troubled" and that she had been praying so long out of her "great anguish and grief."

May we learn to pray in the same way and tell God everything that is on our hearts and in our minds.

The Spirit's help

We do not need to pray aloud. Remember that "Hannah was praying in her heart, and her lips were moving but her voice was not heard" (1

Sam. 1:13). We do not need to formulate beautiful phrases either. Sometimes we cannot find words to express our deepest feelings, but God hears our sighing.

King David was another who certainly was convinced that God is listening. He exclaimed: "All my longings lie open before you, O LORD: my sighing is not hidden from you" (Psalm 38:9). The apostle Paul wrote to the Christians in Rome: "The Spirit helps us in our weakness. We do not know what we ought to pray for, but the Spirit himself intercedes for us with groans that words cannot express" (Rom. 8:26).

When Jesus taught his disciples to pray, you may remember, the model prayer he gave them begins with the words, "Our Father" (Matt. 6:9). When we pray, we are addressing our Father, who loves us and wants the best for us. He wants us to come to him and open up our hearts to him. Jesus said, "your Father, who sees what is done in secret, will reward you" (Matt. 6:6).

Just as Hannah did, we can trust God, our Father, even if we do not see an immediate answer to our prayers or an instant change in our circumstances. *Only believe.*

Rejoicing in the Lord

Can you count on God when nothing seems to go right? Can you trust him when you don't understand? Have you faith in him when all seems dark? The Prophet Habakkuk affirmed (Hab. 3:17,18):

> Though the fig tree does not bud
> > and there are no grapes on the
> > > vines,
> though the olive crop fails
> > and the fields produce no food,
> though there are no sheep in the pen
> > and no cattle in the stalls,
> yet I will rejoice in the LORD,
> > I will be joyful in God my Savior.

Notice that Habakkuk rejoiced in the Lord also in a situation of barrenness, lack, and want. Can you rejoice in the One in whose "presence is fullness of joy" (Psalm 16:11–KJV)?

Hannah was able to rejoice before she saw the answer to her prayers, because her focus had changed. God himself had become the source of her joy, just as he had for Habakkuk. "Rejoice in the Lord always," says the apostle Paul. "I will say it again: Rejoice!" (Phil. 4:4).

10

A Discerning Heart

1 Kings 3:5-14; 2 Chronicles 1:7-12

*I*f God appeared to you and said, "Ask for whatever you want me to give you," I wonder what you would ask for. I suppose that, depending on your needs and your circumstances, you might ask for good health, good looks, a job, a spouse, a child, a home, a holiday, wealth.... The list could go on and on.

Solomon's request

God appeared to King Solomon, and he said, "Ask for whatever you want me to give you" (2 Chron. 1:7). What do you think Solomon asked God for? Solomon had just taken over the throne from his father David; greatly humbled and conscious of his inability to rule over the people with equity, he asked God for "a discerning heart" (1 Kings 3:9). In 2 Chronicles 1:10 it is written that Solomon asked for "wisdom and knowledge" for the same purpose: "to govern this great people." In both cases ("a discerning heart" and "wisdom and knowledge"), the meaning is the same.

Interesting, and all to Solomon's credit, is the altruistic reason for his request—for the good of the people. It was not for his pleasure or advancement. Solomon realized he was dependent on God. He did not try to assume his enormous task in his own strength.

Equipping

Do you feel inadequate at work? Turn to God. Ask him to equip you just as he equipped Solomon for the task he was given. Do you feel you could be a better spouse or parent? Come before the Lord and ask him for what you need. Are you involved in Christian ministry? Draw your strength and understanding from the One who called you in the first place. Surely what we all need in our responsibilities and in our relationships is exactly what Solomon asked God for—"a discerning heart," "wisdom and knowledge."

I often ask the Lord for wisdom and discernment as I counsel people, as I prepare talks and Bible studies, and as I relate with family, friends, and neighbors. A friend, a board member in a Christian mission, recently shared with me that he would have to deal with some problems that had surfaced in that ministry. My instinctive response was that I would pray for wisdom and discernment for him. He said that was exactly what he needed. How wonderful it is to be able to count on God's provision. *Only believe.*

In walking with the Lord, I have been privileged to have close contact with wise Christians gifted with a "discerning heart." When my husband and I began working in Christian ministry, we were greatly encouraged by two people whom I consider the epitome of wisdom and discernment.

One of those friends is a French pastor now in his eighties. The other is an English lady, now ninety, born in China and raised in New Zealand; with her Swiss husband, she worked as a missionary in India with Amy Carmichael before working alongside us in Geneva.

Both of these friends continue to be examples of wise, discerning believers. As I wrote this chapter, I stopped to pray for these two Christians. The Lord has mightily used them as they reflect the light of God's wisdom. Their God-given discernment shines in a dark world, where the truth is often distorted and where values are reversed.

One reason Solomon asked God for wisdom was so that he might be able "to distinguish between right and wrong" (1 Kings 3:9). How we need that same clarity of vision in our twenty-first century post-modern society, where absolutes no longer exist and where everything is relative.

What do you think God thought of Solomon's request? The text tells us: "The Lord was pleased that Solomon had asked for this" (1 Kings 3:10). There is one thing we need never be afraid to ask God for. Indeed, we are encouraged and exhorted to ask him for it. And we have the promise that our prayer will be answered. James tells us: "If any of you lacks wisdom, he should ask God" (James 1:5a). That's straightforward, isn't it? Not only does he tell us to ask for wisdom, but he also assures us that "it will be given."

Let's see what the whole verse says: "If any of you lacks wisdom, he should ask God, who gives generously to all without finding fault, and it will be given to him. But when he asks, he must believe and not doubt...." *Only believe.*

God's answer for Solomon

Because Solomon was not asking in his own interests but for the good of the people, God gave him what he had requested: "I will do what you have asked" (1 Kings 3:12).

Not only did God give Solomon the wisdom and discernment he asked for, but he also gave him way beyond what he had requested. "I will give you wealth, riches and honor" was God's promise to him, and it would be far more than any other king had ever had or ever would possess (2 Chron. 1:12). That is not all. God continued: "If you walk in my ways and obey my statutes and commands as David your father did, I will give you a long life" (1 Kings 3:14).

Have you ever doubted God's generosity? Do you know that he offers you what he gave to Solomon? In fact he offers you *more* than he gave to Solomon. He wants to give you "the riches of his glorious inheritance in the saints" (Eph. 1:18). James wrote: "Has not God chosen those who are poor in the eyes of the world to be rich in faith and to inherit the kingdom he promised those who love him?" (James 2:5). Yes, we are "heirs of God and co-heirs with Christ" (Rom. 8:17).

Treasures in heaven

There is something much more valuable than material wealth; it will last not only for this life, but for the whole of eternity.

Do you remember Jesus' words to his disciples?

> Do not store up for yourselves treasures on earth, where moth and rust destroy, and where thieves break in and steal. But store up for yourselves treasures in heaven, where moth and rust do not destroy, and where thieves do not break in and steal. For where your treasure is, there your heart will be also (Matt. 6:19-21).

I wonder where your treasure is. I know mine is in heaven.

Jesus spoke about how God provides. Note that Jesus referred to Solomon—"Therefore I tell you, do not be anxious about your life, what you shall eat or what you shall drink, nor about your body, what you shall put on. Is not life more than food, and the body more than clothing? Look at the birds of the air: they neither sow nor reap nor gather into barns, and yet your heavenly Father feeds them. Are you not of more value than they? ...And why are you anxious about clothing? Consider the lilies of the field, how they grow; they neither toil nor spin; yet I tell you, even Solomon in all his glory was not arrayed like one of these. But if God so clothes the grass of the field, which today is alive and tomorrow is thrown into the oven, will he not much more clothe you, O men of little faith? (Matt. 6:25-30-RSV)!

Paul longed for Christians to know the treasures that are in Christ. He wrote to the Ephesians, "That out of his glorious riches he may strengthen you with power through his Spirit in your inner being" (Eph. 3:16); he wrote to the Philippians, "My God will meet all your needs according to his glorious riches in Christ Jesus" (Phil. 4:19); and he desired that the Colossians would "...have all the riches of assured understanding and the knowledge of God's mystery, of Christ, in whom are hid all the treasures of wisdom and knowledge" (Col. 2:2,3-RSV). All these treasures and riches are ours too in Jesus! Did you know you possessed such wealth? *Only believe.*

Eternal life

As mentioned earlier, God promised Solomon long life. What kind of life does God promise the believer in Jesus Christ?

Jesus himself gives us the answer: "For God so loved the world that he gave his only Son, that whoever believes in him should not perish but have eternal life" (John 3:16-RSV).

The apostle Paul endorsed this: "The gift of God is eternal life in Christ Jesus our Lord" (Rom. 6:23). The believer is promised not just long life, but eternal life. And "eternal" does not just mean everlasting. It is a new quality of life; it is God's life lived out in the believer now on this earth and for the whole of eternity.

As we have already pointed out, the long life that God promised Solomon was conditional on his obedience (see 1 Kings 3:14). It would be like a reward or a prize for following in his father's footsteps.

The New Testament too talks about rewards, crowns, and prizes for the believer. Paul exclaimed: "I press on towards the goal to win the prize for which God has called me heavenward in Christ Jesus" (Phil. 3:14).

I trust you will take up the challenge of this final exhortation: "Whatever you do, work at it with all your heart, as working for the Lord, not for men, since you know that you will receive an inheritance from the Lord as a reward" (Col. 3:23,24). *Only believe.*

'O LORD, God of heaven, the great and
awesome God, who keeps his covenant of
love with those who love him and obey
his command, let your ear be attentive and
your eyes open to hear the prayer your
servant is praying before you day and night....'

Nehemiah 1:5,6

11

Ashamed and Disgraced

Ezra 9:6-15; Nehemiah 1:5-11

Repentance

Repentance is a subject that concerns all of us without exception, "for all have sinned," as the apostle Paul wrote to the Christians in Rome (Rom. 3:23). Sin separates us from God. "Your iniquities have separated you from your God," exclaimed the prophet Isaiah (Isa. 59:2). We can, however, count on God's forgiveness and cleansing if we turn away from our sin and turn back to God. Such a step is called repentance.

"You shall have no other gods before me," says God (Ex. 20:3). Reading through the Old Testament, I notice that idolatry was the sin that especially caused God to grieve and that led to the downfall of his people. Idolatry is the sin God punishes most severely. In the Old Testament, God's people's alliances with pagan nations, no doubt advantageous politically, invariably resulted in the adoption of pagan rites. These religious observances included idol worship, fertility cults, human sacrifices—all abhorrent to the one true, holy God who had made it clear to his people that they should have no other gods apart from him.

A long time ago, my husband and I started a weekly meeting for French teenagers in our home. They would come for a meal, after which we would sing together, accompanied by a guitar, and then we would study the Bible with them. A modified version of this outreach continued for many years, over which time some of the young people married and continued to attend as couples. One such couple was Pierre and Véronique. Sometimes, particularly when their children were young, they would host the meeting.

Recently Véronique phoned us in tears to tell us that Pierre had left her after twenty-three years of marriage and had gone off with her best friend. We sensed her pain, her feelings of rejection, abandonment, humiliation, betrayal, and loneliness.

Unfaithfulness of God's people

God felt the same kind of pain when his people were unfaithful to him. He likened idolatry to adultery and prostitution. The Old Testament prophetic books are full of evocative descriptions of the unfaithfulness of God's people and of the suffering this caused him. The prophets wept as they delivered their message of judgment. All of Hosea's prophecy is an acted-out real life drama intended to awaken the conscience of God's people by making them realize that "the land is guilty of the vilest adultery in departing from the Lord" (Hos. 1:2). Through the mouth of his prophet Micah, God expressed his grief: "I will weep and wail" (Mic. 1:8).

We would do well to search our own hearts to see which idols we may be worshiping. What or who is the focus of my attention? To what or to whom do my otherwise unoccupied thoughts invariably turn? What or who takes the place of God in my life?

Confession

Ezra and Nehemiah, involved in the rebuilding of Jerusalem after the exile, give us examples of prayers of repentance. In each case, they associate themselves with their people, an idolatrous nation.

Repentance involves confession. Nehemiah began his prayer by confessing the sins of his people: "I confess the sins we Israelites, including myself and my father's house, have committed against you. We have acted very wickedly towards you. We have not obeyed the commands, decrees and laws you gave your servant Moses" (Neh.1:6b,7).

Notice that Nehemiah did not have a condemning attitude towards his people. On the contrary, he identified completely with them in their sin and disgrace. In fact, just before beginning his prayer, he said: "I sat down and wept...I mourned and fasted and prayed" (Neh. 1:4).

Ezra was so completely broken up by the way the people had sinned that he hardly dared to face the Lord: "O my God," he prayed, "I am too ashamed and disgraced to lift up my face to you, my God, because our sins are higher than our heads and our guilt has reached to the heavens" (Ezra 9:6).

Before beginning his prayer, Ezra, like Nehemiah, gave vent to his grief and distress: "I tore my tunic and cloak, pulled hair from my head and beard and sat down appalled" (Ezra 9:3). The sin that caused him such grief was the intermarriage of the Israelites with neighbors who practiced offensive idolatries.

He confessed to God that their evil deeds had brought their calamities upon them (see Ezra 9:13). When the people saw him "praying and confessing, weeping and throwing himself down before the house of God" (Ezra 10:1), they became conscious of their own sin and repented.

Gravity of sin

I wonder if we are as conscious as Ezra and Nehemiah of the gravity of our sin? I read different instances in the Old Testament where God's people sinned against him; and it strikes me that if we took more notice of the extreme severity of the punishment, surely we wouldn't take sin so lightly.

All through the book of Judges we read that, "the Israelites did evil in the eyes of the Lord and served the Baals. They forsook the Lord...They followed and worshiped various gods of the peoples around them" (Judges 2:11,12). God was angry and he punished them, by handing them over to raiders who plundered them. Then he sold them to their enemies, and he made sure they were defeated in all the battles they fought (see Judges 2:14,15).

"They were in great distress," we are told; so the Lord raised up judges who delivered them; but they still "prostituted themselves to other gods and worshipped them" (Judges 2:15b,17). And so it went. Every time they were persecuted and oppressed the Lord would step in and deliver them through his judge, because of his compassion for them.

"But when the judge died, the people returned to ways even more corrupt than those of their fathers, following other gods and serving and worshiping them. They refused to give up their evil practices and stubborn ways" (Judges 2:19).

Fickle, false, and faithless

This returning to sin happened time and time again. God eventually refused to deliver them any more. "Go and cry out to the gods you have chosen," he said. "Let them save you when you are in trouble" (Judges 10:14). How awful if that had been the end of the story!

I am not saying that God would not have been perfectly justified in abandoning his people. After all, they had tried his patience time and time again. They proved to be fickle, false, and faithless.

But doesn't Jeremiah remind us that, "The steadfast love of the Lord never ceases, his mercies never come to an end" (Lam. 3:22-New Revised Standard Version)? At the first signs of repentance from his people, once again God delivered them, as he "could bear Israel's misery no longer" (Judges 10:16).

"The wages of sin is death," wrote the apostle Paul (Rom. 6:23a). I deserve God's judgment and his punishment, just like his people of old. I deserve to die because of my sin. But just as God delivered Israel, so he delivered me. Jesus, the sinless One, willingly took my sin upon himself and bore the punishment in my place, so that I might be forgiven and go free. He paid the penalty. He died instead of me. He gave me life—eternal life.

"If we confess our sins, he is faithful and just and will forgive us our sins and purify us from all unrighteousness" (1 John 1:9). *Only believe.*

Turning to God

I was a child in Zambia when I first heard the gospel. Two new girls, twins called Anne and Elizabeth, appeared one day in my class at school. At break we clustered around them. "Where are you from? What are you doing here in Lusaka?" we asked.

I learned that their parents were missionaries. Soon they began children's meetings in their home and invited me to attend. The twins and I became fast friends. We were the same age, and we would spend a lot of time together, at school and at each other's homes or riding our bikes through the bush. They would talk to me about

Jesus and how he had come to earth to save people.

What does this word "salvation" mean, I wondered? I wasn't very sure of the meaning of a verse that the twins' mother showed me in her Bible one afternoon. As I prepared to go home after playing with Anne and Elizabeth on the swing in their yard, she showed me: "If you confess with your mouth, 'Jesus is Lord,' and believe in your heart that God raised him from the dead, you will be saved" (Rom. 10:9).

Then I realized that being "saved" meant that God would forgive my sins. Even though I understood little else at that point, I went home that day and told God I was sorry for my sin and that I believed, and I thanked him for saving me.

"Repent, then, and turn to God, so that your sins may be wiped out" (Acts 3:19).

Consider him who endured such opposition
from sinful men, so that you will not
grow weary and lose heart.

Hebrews 12:3

12

How Long?

Psalm 123:1-4

Waiting

D o you sometimes get the impression you are always waiting—for something? You go shopping and stand in line at the supermarket check-out counter. You wait for the bus to arrive. You get stuck in a traffic jam. You hang around at the station until the train comes in. You pace up and down at the airport because the plane is late. You sit in the doctor's waiting room. You stand in line to buy tickets for a movie. And your cry goes up: "How long?"

Or you may be waiting for exam results, either academic exams or medical tests. You might be expecting a phone call that never seems to come. You might be waiting for an e-mail, a letter, or a package. You might be separated from loved ones and "can't wait" to be reunited. "How long?"

You are not the first person to have articulated those words, "How long?" The prophet Habakkuk thought that God was never going to respond to him: "How long, O LORD, must I call for help, but you do not listen?" (Hab. 1:2).

The psalms are full of instances where the psalmist utters that cry. In the first two verses of Psalm 13, for example, David exclaims, "How long, O LORD? Will you forget me forever? How long will you hide your face from me? How long must I wrestle with my thoughts and every day have sorrow in my heart? How long will my enemy triumph over me?" David also affirmed: "I waited patiently for the LORD" (Psalm 40:1). The prophet Hosea exhorted God's people to "wait for your God always" (Hos. 12:6b).

Where to look

The psalmist lifted up his eyes to God. He knew where to look. He wrote: "Our eyes look to the LORD our God" (Psalm 123:2). Whatever our situation, whether we are in need or have plenty, when we are in distress, when faced with doubts or uncertainty, that is the One to look to! Looking to God is how we learn the contentment that the apostle Paul wrote about.

I have asked the Lord to teach me to be content, because Paul made clear that contentment is something that has to be learned. I may learn to be content in a given situation, and then the circumstances change, and I have to start learning all over again.

But Paul had "learned to be content *whatever the circumstances*" (Phil. 4:11, emphasis added), That is because he constantly looked to the Lord. For that reason he could say, "I can do everything through him who gives me strength" (Phil. 4:13).

"Let us fix our eyes on Jesus," exhorted the writer to the Hebrews (Heb.12:2). Do you have this same impulse to look to the Lord? May my eyes remain fixed on him! On reading Psalm 123 recently, I exclaimed, "Lord, I want to look to you today, and never take my eyes off you!"

Those thoughts were forming in my mind one Sunday morning before I went to church, as I sat reading in Colossians 3. One verse seemed to leap off the page at me: "Set your minds on things above, not on earthly things" (Col. 3:2), rendered in the Jerusalem Bible as "Let your thoughts be on heavenly things, not on the things that are on the earth." This underlined where my concentration should be.

Psalm 123 says: "Our eyes look to the LORD our God till he shows us his mercy." When will that be? How long? "Wait for the LORD," replied David; "be strong and take heart and wait for the LORD" (Psalm 27:14). And again, "Be still before the LORD and wait patiently for him...Wait for the LORD and keep his way" (Psalm 37:7,34). In Psalm 119:166, we read, "I wait for your salvation, O LORD." But we don't like waiting! How long, O Lord, how long?

Hope and expectation

Waiting, as it is expressed in the Bible, is not a mournful resignation. It is, rather, a joyful anticipation and expectation. It seems to be synonymous with the word "hope," and the hope expressed in the Scriptures is in fact a blessed assurance.

> I wait for the LORD, my soul waits, and in his word I put my hope. My soul waits for the Lord more than watchmen wait for the morning, more than watchmen wait for the morning. O Israel, put your hope in the LORD, for with the LORD is unfailing love and with him is full redemption. (Psalm 130:5-7).

Note how the psalmist repeated: "...more than watchmen wait for the morning...." The hope expressed is an absolute certainty.

Just as the watchman knows that morning will indeed come, so the believer is sure that God will indeed act. In fact, the Christian's anticipation is even greater than that of the watchman.

Longing for eternity

Another song of God's people waiting to see God's mercy in the light of ridicule is Psalm 123. They have endured contempt from the proud and arrogant. Surely the longing and waiting are symptomatic of their desire to be free from the burdens of this life. Deep down it is a longing for eternity, for being in the very presence of God.

Yes, there may be things in this life that we yearn for with the same desperation for our desires to be satisfied: the desire to get married, the desire to have children, the desire for good health, and many other understandable desires.

All are legitimate longings, but all are shadows of that one, deep, all-pervasive desire for God.

In fact, Psalm 42:1 expresses longing in this way: "As the deer pants for streams of water, so my soul pants for you, O God. My soul thirsts for God, for the living God." Similar thoughts are expressed by David in Psalm 63:1: "O God, you are my God, earnestly I seek you; my soul thirsts for you, my body longs for you, in a dry and weary land where there is no water."

According to the letter to the Hebrews, people who acknowledge that they are "aliens and strangers on earth...show that they are looking for a country of their own" (Heb. 11:13,14). Abraham was "looking forward to the city with foundations, whose architect and builder is God" (Heb.11:10). So are we looking forward, and we will not be fully satisfied until we get there. However, we still have to live this life on earth in the meantime. It is a life of faith, looking to the Lord our God and waiting for him. *Only believe.*

To you, O LORD, I lift up my soul;
in you I trust, O my God.

Psalm 25:1,2a

13

Focus

Psalm 25:1-22

$\mathcal{I}$ n our multi-ethnic, multi-cultural church in Geneva, Switzerland, we enjoyed over the years several "International Evenings." Those times of fellowship were great fun. The church hall was usually decorated with flags representing the different countries. People came in national dress and provided delicious food from their country as well as music or other entertainment.

Dangerous activity

At one such evening organized by the young adults of the church, the contingent from the Philippines was particularly creative. They introduced the Tinikling dance, whereby two thick, long bamboo poles were placed parallel to each other on the floor. Two people, one person at each end, grabbed the poles, one in each hand,

and rhythmically and repeatedly banged the poles together and separated them while dancers lithely and nimbly wrought intricate steps in and out between the poles, barely avoiding having their feet smashed each time the poles clashed together.

I was forcibly "volunteered" to engage in the Tinikling dance, which looked to me like a very dangerous activity! So it was in fear and trembling that I climbed onto the platform in front of a large audience and began to try to copy the footwork of my Filipino partner, while keeping my eyes fixed warily on the poles at my feet.

After clumsily hopping and jumping over those heavy threatening pieces of wood for a while, I suddenly realized that my partner was talking to me. He had in fact been trying to get my attention for some time, but I was so focused on the bamboo poles, on my feet, and on the potential harm and danger, that I had not even noticed that he was speaking!

I gradually became aware of his voice and of what he was saying. He had been repeating over and over again, "Don't look at the bamboo; look at me. Don't look at the bamboo; look at me."

Look!

As I eventually managed to succeed in taking my gaze off what represented danger for me, and finally was able to look my partner in the eye, I was steadied by his look. No longer focusing on my feet and the bamboo poles, I could keep in rhythm and avoid an accident.

I thought afterwards: how often do we focus on the difficulties and dangers of life rather than on the Lord? It is so easy to center our gaze on our problems and become obsessed with them.

In chapter eight of this book, we have already seen how Hannah's focus changed and how God himself became the source of her joy. In chapter twelve, we referred to Hebrews 12:2, where we are exhorted to "fix our eyes on Jesus." We also looked at Psalm 123, where the psalmist lifts up his eyes to the Lord and affirms, "our eyes look to the LORD our God" (Psalm 123:2b).

That is what David also does in Psalm 25. He certainly has problems. He talks about his enemies and writes that he is "lonely and afflicted," referring to "troubles of [his] heart," as well as to his affliction and his distress (Psalm 25:16,17).

Yet he doesn't put his difficulties at the center of his thoughts. On the contrary, he turns to God. "To you, O LORD, I lift up my soul; in you I trust, O my God" are the opening words of this psalm.

What better beginning could there be than that? Later he makes a point of saying, "My eyes are ever on the LORD" (Psalm 25:15).

Your eyes?

Where is your focus? Can you echo those words: "My eyes are ever on the LORD"? If only we could keep our eyes fixed on Jesus at all times! Remember the words of the Filipino dancer during the Tinikling dance: "Don't look at the bamboo; look at me." I translated those words into: "Don't focus on the problem; look to the Lord."

Many are familiar with the way "look" figured so strongly in Charles Haddon Spurgeon's conversion experience. Because of a snowstorm one Sunday morning, he entered a small Primitive Methodist Chapel. Due to the bad weather, the minister did not turn up, and few others were there, either.

Spurgeon wrote: "At last, a very thin-looking man...went up into the pulpit to preach." Spurgeon thought he seemed "really stupid," and "was obliged to stick to his text, for the simple reason that he had little else to say."

However, the preacher constantly repeated the words: "Look unto me, and be ye saved, all the ends of the earth" (Isa. 45:22–KJV). He directly addressed the young Spurgeon and exhorted him to "look to Jesus Christ. Look! Look! Look!" Spurgeon later wrote that he "saw at once the way of salvation." He said: "I looked until I could almost have looked my eyes away.... That precious text led me to the cross of Christ. I can testify that the joy of that day was utterly indescribable."

Whatever your need at any time, look to Jesus, keep him as your focal point, and trust him—for your salvation, deliverance, forgiveness, and cleansing; for new life, sanctification, fulfillment, provision, and direction; for comfort, consolation, rest, peace, and strength; and to uphold, equip, and protect you. Look! *Only believe.*

14

Unfailing Love

Psalm 143

Does it ever happen to you that a passage of Scripture speaks to you so deeply and strikes you so hard that you feel overwhelmed? There wells up in you excitement, eagerness, hunger, and thirst to enter more deeply into the mind and purposes of God. You long for a closer and more intimate relationship with him.

It is probably similar to what the two disciples felt on the road to Emmaus, where their hearts were "burning" within them (Luke 24:32) while Jesus opened up the Scriptures to them.

Something like that once happened to me while reading Psalm 143.

Freedom to approach God

The first thing that got me excited—possibly because I used to be a language teacher—was the number of imperative verbs! Now, imperative verbs may not thrill you a bit! But they did thrill me. There are eleven affirmative and two negative imperatives in the New International Version of the Bible.

However, don't worry; it was not the grammar that most excited me, but the fact that the imperatives emphasize the psalmist's freedom in approaching God in prayer. You see, each imperative in Psalm 143 is a specific prayer request.

We can tend to be vague, imprecise, and *un*-specific in the way we pray; but God wants us to give him our specific requests. He wants us to bring our needs to him as David did.

Faithful and righteous

David's prayer in Psalm 143 is not a cry in the wilderness, nor a shout in the void. He knows he is addressing his *imperatives* to God, with whom he already has a relationship.

"*Listen* to my cry for mercy; in your faithfulness and righteousness *come* to my relief" (Psalm 143:1, emphases added). The God he addresses is faithful and righteous—just, pure, and holy. David asks first for mercy, because he realizes that God is righteous.

The apostle Paul addresses the theme of righteousness in his letter to the Romans: "There is no one righteous, not even one.... All have sinned and fall short of the glory of God" (Rom. 3:10,23).

David prayed, "Do not bring your servant into judgment, for no one living is righteous before you" (Psalm 143:2). He threw himself onto

God's mercy. And so can we. Just as David was so vividly aware, we all deserve to come under God's wrath and judgment. Our sin has to be dealt with, "but the gift of God is eternal life in Christ Jesus our Lord" (Rom. 6:23). *Only believe.*

Vanquished foe

Now, let us consider David's main concern. It is an enemy who has put him in a terrible situation of desperate need. David, therefore, cries out to God in the time of need.

What a good example for us to follow, because God can meet all our needs! The apostle Paul states quite categorically to the Philippians: "My God will meet all your needs according to his glorious riches in Christ Jesus" (Phil. 4:19). We also have an encouraging exhortation from the writer of the letter to the Hebrews: "Let us then approach the throne of grace with confidence, so that we may receive mercy and find grace to help us in our time of need" (Heb. 4:16). Let us avail ourselves of this tremendous privilege of bringing all our needs before God in prayer.

"The enemy pursues me..." (Psalm 143:3), David cried. We too have an enemy. "Your enemy the devil," said the apostle Peter, "prowls around like a roaring lion looking for someone to devour" (1 Pet. 5:8). We are to resist our enemy and remember that he is a vanquished foe. In the letter to the Hebrews we read that Jesus shared in our humanity "so that by his death he might destroy him who holds the power of death—that is, the devil" (Heb. 2:14). The apostle John tells us that "the reason the Son of God appeared was to destroy the devil's work" (1 John 3:8).

Counting on God

David suffered greatly because of his enemy: "...my spirit grows faint within me; my heart within me is dismayed...my spirit fails..." (Psalm 143:3,4,7)! Every cry is heavy with meaning and resonates with feelings of extreme suffering. These phrases are reminiscent of what Jesus went through in the Garden of Gethsemane. The prophet Isaiah wrote: "It was the LORD's will to crush him [Jesus] and cause him to suffer" (Isa. 53:10).

Have you ever felt like that—crushed, dismayed, in darkness? You need never feel alone in your suffering. You need never feel less than fully understood. Others have been there before you, like David. Even more, Someone else has been there before you—Jesus, whose suffering was beyond comparison.

"I remember..."

After confiding all his suffering to God, in Psalm 143 David does something that we see quite often in the Scriptures and which is another good example for us to follow.

He turns his mind back to past mercies and past deliverances: "I remember the days of long ago..." (Psalm 143:5). He is drawing courage from what God has already done in his life, as well as in the bigger scene of creation and history. He deliberately brings to mind former answers to prayer, and previous interventions of God; and he takes heart.

Because of what God has already done in the past, David is encouraged to come before him again. He doesn't come in any half-hearted way. "I spread out my hands to you," he exclaims. "My soul thirsts for you like a parched land" (Psalm 143:6). David reaches out his hands to God, wanting to touch him, wanting to receive from him.

He is thirsty for God. He pours out all the longings of his soul and yearnings of his heart. May this be your experience, too. The closer you come to God and the better you know him, the more you remember what he can do and the more you yearn to know him better.

God provides

David mentions God's "unfailing love" (Psalm 143:8). God's love is steadfast and kind. It is faithful to a covenant. There is firm commitment behind it. For this reason David goes on to say, "I have put my trust in you" (Psalm 143:8). He knows he can count on God.

What about you? Have you put your trust in God? Do you have this same assurance? *Only believe.*

Finally, David pleads, "For your name's sake, O LORD, preserve my life" (Psalm 143:11). In God's "name" are brought together all the attributes that we've been talking about—his faithfulness, righteousness, trustworthiness, mercy, and steadfast love. God's whole character is at stake.

David knows that God will not let him down. Indeed God cannot let him down, because God is always consistent with his own character. Therefore, he could pray with assurance.

And you can pray with assurance, too. If you have entered into a covenant relationship with God through Jesus Christ, then you can count on his righteousness, faithfulness, trustworthiness, and steadfast love, just as David did.

If you do not yet know the joy of your sins being forgiven, if you have not yet entered into a relationship with God through Jesus, what is stopping you right now?

Precise requests

We come to the essence of David's prayer—all those imperative verbs I mentioned in the beginning! We have already looked at some of them: *hear, listen, come, preserve,* and the negative imperative: *do not bring.* These are precise requests. Let us once more take example from the psalmist and bring *our* precise requests before God.

Do you know what will happen when you do? The apostle Paul says that when you present your requests to God, "the peace of God, which transcends all understanding will guard your hearts and your minds in Christ Jesus" (Phil. 4:7). What a wonderful promise!

From Psalm 143:7, our verb list gets longer: *answer, do not hide, show me, rescue me, teach me, preserve, bring, silence,* and *destroy.* Through this list of imperative requests, David moves gradually and imperceptibly from his own needs to the fulfillment of God's overall purposes: "Show me the way I should go," and "Teach me to do your will" (Psalm 143:8,10).

Beyond our needs

I think that the time will come when we will begin to look beyond our own needs to God's greater purposes. We must lift our eyes, as Jesus told his disciples to do, and see those fields ripe for harvest, and ask the Lord of the harvest "to send out workers into his harvest field" (Matt. 9:38). As we open our eyes to see our needy world and begin to pray accordingly, our needs and desires may not seem quite so pressing.

David said: "I have put my trust in you" (Psalm 143:8). Let us follow his example. Let us cry out in trust to God, who is faithful and righteous and who loves us with unfailing love.

But you brought my life up from the pit,
O LORD my God.

Jonah 2:6b

15

Saved from an Impossible Situation

Jonah 1-4

I can think of many ways to travel—on foot, by horseback, car, truck, plane, train, bus, RV, motorbike, bicycle, on a camel or an elephant...and you can probably add to the list; but never before have I heard of anyone traveling inside a fish.

Many of us have a special place where we can talk with God in prayer—our study or bedroom, a cozy nook, inside or outside—where we can lay aside our busyness and spend precious time with the Lord. But never before have I heard of anyone praying inside a fish.

But a man named Jonah did both!

Running from God

"From inside the fish Jonah prayed to the LORD his God" (Jonah 2:1). Who is Jonah? Where did the fish come from, and what is Jonah doing inside it? How did he get there?

God sent the fish: "The LORD provided a great fish" (Jonah 1:17). He sent it for one reason only: "to swallow Jonah." Why would God do that? And how did Jonah come to be within swallowing distance of such a big fish?

Jonah had disobeyed God. God had told him to do something that he did not want to do, so he ran. God had said: "Go to the great city of Nineveh..." (Jonah 1:2), yet Jonah went in the exact opposite direction.

Why did Jonah run away? Was he afraid to enter such a wicked city as Nineveh? Did he think that it would be hopeless to preach against it, that the inhabitants were already so far gone as never to want to change? Did he think they deserved all they were going to get, and he wanted to make sure that God would not show mercy to them?

God wanted Jonah to go to Nineveh to preach against the city because of its great wickedness. Instead of that, Jonah "ran away from the LORD and headed for Tarshish" (Jonah 1:3) Have you ever been tempted to run from God? Many people do try. They first try to stifle that still, small voice, by throwing themselves agitatedly into whatever might come their way. Activism and a constant noise preclude any quiet repose when they might hear God speak.

It is easy to get so busy that there is no time to think. Any incipient thoughts about the meaning of life, death, judgment, and life to come are quickly banished and replaced by distractions of all kinds.

Violent storm

Whatever the reason Jonah fled (and it would seem it was to avoid preaching against Nineveh— see Jonah 4:2) "he went down to Joppa, where he found a ship... After paying the fare, he went aboard and sailed for Tarshish" (Jonah 1:3). The text repeats in no uncertain terms the reason for Jonah's trip to Tarshish. He was going there in order "to flee from the LORD."

And on the voyage, "the LORD sent a great wind on the sea, and such a violent storm arose that the ship threatened to break up" (Jonah 1:4). The sailors were terrified and started to throw the cargo overboard in order to lighten the ship.

Quite oblivious to all that was going on, Jonah was fast asleep below deck! That is, until the captain woke him up and told him to pray. Jonah had already explained to the crew that he was running away from God, and they rightly concluded that Jonah's disobedience was the cause of the danger they were now in. "So they asked him, 'What should we do to you to make the sea calm down for us?'" (Jonah 1:11).

Jonah recognized that the storm was indeed his fault, so he courageously told them to pick him up and throw him into the sea. The sailors did all they could to avoid taking such drastic action.

However, "the sea grew even wilder than before" so much so, that they finally complied with Jonah's solution: they "took Jonah and threw him overboard" and then the sea immediately "grew calm" (Jonah 1:13,15).

Thus, Jonah became easy prey for the fish that God provided.

Calling out to God

With no books, magazines, or newspapers; no radio, television, mobile phone, computer or DVD, Jonah remained "inside the fish three days and three nights" (Jonah 1:17). He had plenty of time to think, to meditate, to engage in self-examination, and to pray.

What a situation he was in, drowning in a turbulent sea: "The engulfing waters threatened me, the deep surrounded me; seaweed was wrapped around my head" (Jonah 2:5). In his distress there, Jonah called out to God.

Do you ever think you have done anything so *bad* that you have forfeited having recourse to God? Jonah had disobeyed, run away, and caused a calamity. He had brought all this upon himself. He could easily have thought that there was no point in turning to God. He could have assumed that God would want nothing more to do with him, for he had overstepped the mark.

Yet, as he sank, Jonah's thoughts flew out toward God. God intervened, and Jonah praised him. "You brought my life up from the pit, O LORD my God," he exclaimed. "When my life was ebbing away, I remembered you, LORD, and my prayer rose to you" (Jonah 2:7).

Worthless idols

The three days and three nights that Jonah spent inside the fish gave him just the time he needed to examine himself and sort himself out and realize that he must put God first in his life. "Those who cling to worthless idols," he said, "forfeit the grace that could be theirs. But I, with a song of thanksgiving, will sacrifice to you. What I have vowed I will make good. Salvation comes from the LORD" (Jonah 2:8,9).

When Jonah had finished praying, it says, "the LORD commanded the fish, and it vomited Jonah onto dry land" (Jonah 2:10). Finally, "...the word of the LORD came to Jonah a second time: 'Go to the great city of Nineveh and proclaim to it the message I give you.' Jonah obeyed the word of the LORD and went to Nineveh" (Jonah 3:1-3a). *Only believe.*

Fortunately, Jonah knew he could turn to God when in trouble, even though it was of his own making. I hope you know where to turn as well. There is no sin that is beyond God's grace, mercy, and forgiveness.

If you have turned your back on God, if you have been running away from him and have gotten yourself in a mess, you can come back, confident that he will hear your cry for help. "From the depths of the grave I called for help," says Jonah, "and you listened to my cry" (Jonah 2:2).

Do not think either that it is ever *too late* to come back to God. You may have spent your whole life running away from him, but you can still turn back even at death's door.

Remember the criminal on the cross, who just before dying, cried out, "Jesus, remember me when you come into your kingdom." Jesus replied, "Today you will be with me in paradise" (Luke 23:42,43).

Rescue operation

Like Jonah, David acknowledged the Lord's help, saying, "He lifted me out of the slimy pit, out of the mud and mire; he set my feet on a rock and gave me a firm place to stand" (Psalm 40:2).

Many Christians can testify metaphorically to this same experience. Many hymns have been written on this theme of being rescued from sinking sands and from drowning. This experience is one we all share—this need to cry out to God, to trust him when we are in trouble, to know he will hear and help us.

I remember once trying to explain the concept of salvation to a group of children in Geneva, Switzerland. I likened it to a rescue operation. Instead of a rescue from drowning, I used the illustration of a recent rescue—a disastrous fire in the Mont Blanc tunnel, linking France and Italy, which occurred in 1999.

At that time, an Italian fireman kept returning to the tunnel, going inside, and bringing injured people out. He did this until he finally was overcome and died. He gave his life to save those people!

I told the children that for an eternal salvation, Jesus gave his life to save us all! He died instead of us so that we might live forever. *Only believe.*

May God be at the center of my life. May he also be at the center of your life, no matter what you have done or how far away you have run from him—as he later was the center of Jonah's life.

16

Power

Ephesians 1:17-23; 3:14-19

*P*ower, strength, authority, and dominion—we often hear these words. In the world's view, power is a quite fashionable concept. We hear of power in politics, economics, business, sports, and human relationships. As the world sees it, power is what counts.

Abuse of power

Yet, worldly power leads almost inevitably to its abuse. We see that abuse in all areas of life. Power enables us to tread others underfoot as we make our way to the top.

How often do we hear on the news reports of child abuse or some other form of abuse? As I was writing this chapter, I heard on the news of two French teenagers who tortured an octogenarian for over thirty hours in order to steal from him the paltry sum of forty euros, approximately forty dollars. The man later died of his injuries. The adolescents, when questioned, admitted their crime with no signs of remorse.

The apostle Paul spelled out to the young man, Timothy, what people would be like "in the last days," and it is not pleasant reading. He wrote:

> People will be lovers of themselves, lovers of money, boastful, proud, abusive, disobedient to their parents, ungrateful, unholy, without love, unforgiving, slanderous, without self-control, brutal, not lovers of the good, treacherous, rash, conceited, lovers of pleasure rather than lovers of God—having a form of godliness, but denying its power (2 Tim. 3:2-5).

"Incomparably great power"

In two of the apostle Paul's powerful prayers in a letter to believers in Ephesus, chapters one and three, appear words relative to power. The prayers greatly inspire us, because the depth of their meaning goes beyond what our minds can fully grasp. Yet, we can glean much from them, knowing that all the blessings of God's power, asked for in the prayers, are available to us in Christ.

The apostle Paul prayed for the Ephesians to know the power which is infinitely greater than the despotism of worldly power described in 2 Timothy. It is the power set to work by God, truly to work *for* us, not against us, for our good. Paul said that this "incomparably great power" is "for us who believe" (Eph. 3:19), and he prayed that we might experience it.

To help us understand something of this incredible power, Paul described it as being "like the working of his [God's] mighty strength, which he exerted in Christ when he raised him from the dead" (Eph.1:19-20). The same power that God displayed with all his strength at the resurrection of Jesus is put to work for you and me! *Only believe.*

How can we possibly grasp the full depth of meaning of such a statement? Through his Spirit, God enables us to understand and assimilate the marvelous truths that are beyond our natural comprehension. Paul wrote: "I keep asking that the God of our Lord Jesus Christ, the glorious Father, may give you the Spirit of wisdom and revelation, so that you may know him better" (Eph. 3:17). We need to be enlightened by the Holy Spirit in order to understand the things of God.

Why did Paul pray that we might experience the "incomparably great power" of the Holy Spirit? So we can compete with those who wield power in this world? So we can lord it over those who dominate and domineer?

On the contrary, when we are most conscious of our own inherent weakness is when we can appropriate God's power. Remember what God said to the apostle Paul: "My power is made perfect in weakness" (2 Cor. 12:9). And Paul responded: "When I am weak, then I am strong" (2 Cor. 12:10b).

Ray Harrison was a founding member of the church in Geneva, Switzerland, where my husband ministered for over thirty years. In his little devotional book, *Situation Psalms,* he wrote that Goliath was insulted when David went out to fight against him. After all, David had refused Saul's armor and went to meet Goliath armed only with his sling and five stones (see 1 Sam. 17:38-40).

Although weak, David counted on the Lord's strength. "I come against you in the name of the LORD Almighty," he said (1 Sam. 17:45). We read that, "David triumphed over the Philistine with a sling and a stone; without a sword in his hand he struck down the Philistine and killed him" (1 Sam. 17:50).

However, David did not glory in this victory. As Ray Harrison wrote, "He wasn't out to prove that he was the better warrior." No, David's concern was that God should have all the glory. "The whole world will know that there is a God in Israel," he declared (1 Sam. 17: 46b).

"Strong in the Lord"

Paul encouraged other believers to find their strength in God. To the Christians in Ephesus he wrote: "Be strong in the Lord and in his mighty power" (Eph. 6:10). But even Christians can be taken in and can fall into a trap.

Much has been said about the power of the Holy Spirit. Why do I want so much to experience the power of the Spirit? So that I can stand out as a better Christian than others? So that I can perform signs and wonders? Jesus said, "Be careful not to do your 'acts of righteousness' before men, to be seen by them" (Matt. 6:1).

It is all very subtle. Do you want power? Do you pray for power? Why? So that you can be as ruthless and as ambitious as others in this world? Or so that you can be like Jesus, humble, caring and loving, and so that you can understand and experience the unlimited dimensions of his love?

Better way

Do I want the Holy Spirit to make me more like Jesus, who "humbled himself and became obedient to death—even death on a cross!" (Phil. 2:8)? In the world, there is a spirit of competition and rivalry to get ahead, be the best, reach the summit of a profession, and be admired by others.

The Word of God teaches us a different and better way: "Do nothing out of selfish ambition or vain conceit, but in humility consider others better than yourselves" (Phil. 2:3). In his prayer recorded in Ephesians 3:14-19 (which we examined in the previous book of this series, *Seeking God's Face*), Paul prayed that believers may be strengthened "with power" (Eph. 3:16). Why? "So that Christ may dwell in [their] hearts through faith," and that they might grasp something of the dimensions of God's love (Eph. 3:17-19), which goes way beyond our human comprehension.

Only through the power of the Holy Spirit can we really grasp these deep things of God. Let us appropriate the words of these prayers in

Ephesians 1 and 3. Let us trust that God will abundantly answer. *Only believe.*

"Now to him who is able to do immeasurably more than all we ask or imagine, according to his power that is at work within us, to him be glory in the church and in Christ Jesus throughout all generations, for ever and ever! Amen" (Eph. 3:20,21).

17

God's Touch

Revelation 4:11

Beautiful creation

Have you ever gotten up early and gone out to watch the sun come up? Some years ago, during a mountain holiday in Switzerland, I did just that. I went out into a silent, gray world devoid of all color and gradually saw one snowy peak after the other turn pink. Alone in the Alps, I felt that the whole world was mine and that this magnificent spectacle was just for me.

It seemed to me that this glorious sight would have been wasted had there been no human eye to behold it. And yet, had I not been there, the sun would have risen just the same.

We know from the book of Revelation that God himself takes pleasure in the beauty of his creation. Some of the older versions of our Bibles read as follows: "Thou art worthy, O Lord, to receive glory and honour and power: for thou hast created all things, and for thy pleasure they are and were created" (Rev. 4:11–KJV). Even though the phrase translated "for thy pleasure" in the above quotation, would probably be more correctly rendered "by thy pleasure," in other words "by your will" (see NIV), the alternative translation is true as well.

God's generosity

The glory of the sunrise, whether observed by human eye or not, spoke to me of God's generosity, over-abundance, and lavishness of giving.

The Bible[*] tells us that God gives not just life, but *abundant* life (John 10:10). He "*richly* provides us with everything for our enjoyment" (1 Tim. 6:17). His love "*surpasses* knowledge" (Eph. 3:19). He is able to do "*immeasurably more* than all we ask or imagine" (Eph. 3:20). The peace he gives "*transcends* all understanding" (Phil. 4:7).

The psalmist exclaimed, "You have made known to me the path of life; you will fill me with joy in your presence, with *eternal pleasures* at your right hand" (Psalm 16:11). All you have to do is to put out your hand and receive God's gracious, abundant provision. *Only believe.*

"Gentle whisper"

The mountain glory I witnessed at sunrise spoke to me of another aspect of God's character. When I saw the peaks suffused in that rosy glow, I felt there should be a loud trumpet blast or a great

---

[*] emphases added

acclamation to herald the new day. I couldn't believe that what was taking place before my eyes was happening so silently, unobtrusively, and in such peace and tranquility.

Isn't that typical of the way God works? When he appeared to Elijah, we read that there was "a great and powerful wind...but the LORD was not in the wind. After the wind there was an earthquake, but the LORD was not in the earthquake. After the earthquake came a fire, but the LORD was not in the fire. And after the fire came a gentle whisper" (1 Kings 19:11,12). God revealed himself to Elijah in "a gentle whisper," or in a "still small voice" (RSV).

Don't we still see God at work today in the same quiet, discreet way, through his Holy Spirit in the lives of believers? You notice if you are looking in the right direction! Had I not actually been looking at the peaks in question, nothing would have told me about this glory that was unfolding in my presence. Likewise, the results of the Holy Spirit's transforming work in the lives of God's children can be spectacular as believers are changed into the likeness of Jesus Christ and are equipped to serve him.

Just as I stepped out into a gray world that was transformed by the touch of God's paintbrush, so our lives—which may be colorless and drab—can be transformed into things of beauty by God's touch upon them.

"Eternal light"

Recently, I witnessed another sunrise, this time at the coast in New South Wales, Australia, with a close and trusted friend with whom I have experienced times of precious fellowship and deep communion. We watched the sun rise over the horizon and shed a golden path of light across the Pacific Ocean. The light and warmth of the sun's rays reminded us of God's holiness and love. "In light inaccessible, hid from our eyes," wrote Walter Chalmers Smith of this God whose "eyes are too pure to look on evil" (Hab. 1:13).

God has made himself accessible by paying the penalty for our sin and dying in our place, because he loves us. As we contemplated the "eternal light" as reflected in the rising sun and remembered the offering and sacrifice which opened up the way for us to enter God's presence, we marveled anew that

> The sons of ignorance and night
> May dwell in the eternal light
> Through the eternal love.
> —Thomas Binney

18

Glory!

John 17:1-5, 20-26

C hapter 17 of John's gospel is a prayer of Jesus. His time on earth was drawing to a close. He prayed: "Father, the time has come" (John 17:1a). The time had come for what? For Jesus to be crucified. Jesus then prayed, "Glorify your Son, that your Son may glorify you" (John 17:1b). How was Jesus glorified, and how did he bring glory to his Father?

What do you think of when you hear the word "glory"? Does it convey splendor, majesty, radiance, effulgence, and shining light? Actually, it could mean all or any of those things. In the New Testament, the Greek word "doxa" (translated "glory" in English) means the outshining of the inner being and is chiefly used to describe the revelation of the character and presence of God as seen in the person and work of Jesus Christ.

At the cross

In the Old Testament, Moses said to God, "Show me your glory" (Ex. 33:18), and God replied, "...you cannot see my face, for no one may see me and live....When my glory passes by, I will put you in a cleft in the rock and cover you with my hand until I have passed by" (Ex. 33:20,22). In 1 Timothy 6:16, Paul wrote about God "who lives in unapproachable light, whom no one has seen or can see."

Yet God, whom no one had seen or could see, revealed himself in his Son Jesus Christ. "No one has ever seen God. It is God the only Son, who is close to the Father's heart, who has made him known" (John 1:18-NRSV). Here John is referring to the incarnation—the fact that God became man in the form of Jesus and thereby made himself known to man. "And the Word [Jesus] became flesh and lived among us, and we have seen his glory" (John 1:14-NRSV).

Leon Morris, in his commentary on the Gospel of John, writes that here "John is speaking of that glory that was seen in the literal, physical Jesus of Nazareth. As he came in lowliness we have an example of the paradox...that the true glory is to be seen, not in the outward splendor, but in the lowliness with which the Son of God lived for men and suffered for them...It is the cross of shame that manifests his true glory."

When he entered Jerusalem for the Passover, Jesus predicted his own death. He said: "The hour has come for the Son of Man to be glorified" (John 12:23). And he prayed, "Father, glorify your name!" (John 12:28). Jesus looks for glory in the *last* place that men would seek it—at the cross!

"It is finished"

In the hours before his death, Jesus was betrayed by Judas, denied by Peter, buffeted by the High Priest's officials, flogged by the Roman governor, crowned with a ring of thorns, mocked by the crowd, and abused by the soldiers. Then he was nailed to the cross. Just before bowing his head and giving up his spirit, Jesus said, "It is finished" (John 19:30). Was this a sigh of relief that all his suffering was over? Or did his words have another meaning?

Before he said, "It is finished," we read that Jesus knew "that all was now completed, and so that the Scripture would be fulfilled..." (John 19:28). The words "completed" and "fulfilled" are significant in our understanding of Jesus' statement, "It is finished."

Surely he was saying that he had finished the work he came to do; he had accomplished the ministry for which he was destined; he had fulfilled the purpose for which he became man. So rather than a sigh of relief, the statement was an expression of satisfaction, perhaps almost a cry of victory: "It is finished!" "I've done it!" And this is the way Jesus' prayer, to be glorified and thereby to bring glory to God, was answered. Does it seem strange to you that it was at the cross, a place of shame, that God was glorified?

Faithful followers of Christ

Jesus was glorified at the cross. Where then does our glory lie? To find out, we need to return to Jesus' prayer in John 17.

After praying for himself and his disciples, Jesus said: "I pray also for those who will believe in me through their message" (John 17:20). I always get such a thrill when I read that, because it means that Jesus prayed for you and for me, for those of us who have come to faith through the apostolic message. He prayed that we might love one another and be united. Then he said, "I have given them the glory that you gave me..." (verse 22).

Glory as the world understands it is often equated with fame, prestige, celebrity, money, status, position, and possessions. Jesus had none of these. He didn't even have a "place to lay his head" (Matt. 8:20). If we are to be faithful followers of Christ, we are to live in contradiction to what the world thinks, teaches, and aspires to.

A few years ago I spent a few days alone in a small apartment in the Swiss Alps. I had gone away tired and irritable; things were getting on top of me; I was beginning to resent some of the demands being made upon me and some of the things I was expected to do. I looked upon this break in my schedule as a time when I could listen to God. I asked God to speak to me and he did, through Jesus' prayer in John 17.

God enabled me to see my daily grind as service to others and therefore to him. He gave me a different perspective on life. He helped me to see what I call "the glorious in the mundane."

Our eternal glory

Do you remember when Jesus said, "If anyone would come after me, he must deny himself and take up his cross daily and follow me" (Luke 9:23)? Well, that's where our glory lies, in dying to ourselves and giving him first place in our lives, in following him and seeking to do his will. For us, true glory lies in the path of lowly service, wherever that might lead. It could lead to persecution. It could even lead to death.

But death is not the end. With the eyes of faith, we can look beyond the sufferings of this life to that "eternal glory" (2 Cor. 4:17) that will be ours in heaven. We can anticipate with assurance those "eternal pleasures at [God's] right hand" (Psalm 16:11). We can know without a doubt that in God's presence "there will be no more death or mourning or crying or pain" (Rev. 21:4). What a wonderful assurance! What hope! What victory! What glory!

Only believe.

Bibliography

Binney, Thomas (1797-1874). Hymn: "Eternal Light! Eternal Light!" (*page 114*)

Douglas, J.D. Organizing Editor, *The New Bible Dictionary*. London, England: Inter-Varsity Press, 1962.

Fernando, Ajith. *Jesus Driven Ministry*. Wheaton, Illinois: Crossway Books, 2002: 225. (*page 34*)

Harrison, Ray. *Situation Psalms*. Tauranga, New Zealand: The International Needs Network, 2002: 149, 150. (*page 108*)

Kidner, Derek. *Psalms 1-72: An Introduction and Commentary of Books I and II of the Psalms*. London, England: Inter-Varsity Press, 1973: 115-117.

Kidner, Derek. *Psalms 73-150: A Commentary on Books III, IV and V of the Psalms*. London England: Inter-Varsity Press, 1975: 475, 476.

Morris, Leon. *Luke: An Introduction and Commentary*. London, England: Inter-Varsity Press, 1974: 138. (*page 21*)

Morris, Leon. *The Gospel According to John*. Grand Rapids, Michigan: Eerdmans, 1975: 104. (*page 116*)

Smith, Walter Chalmers (1824-1908). Hymn: "Immortal, Invisible, God Only Wise" (*page 114*)

Spurgeon, Charles Haddon. *The Early Years, 1834-1859: A Revised Edition of His Autobiography*. Originally compiled by his wife and private secretary. London, England: The Banner of Truth Trust, 1967: 87, 88. (*pages 89,90*)

Stigers, Harold G. *A* Commentary on Genesis. Grand Rapids, Michigan: Zondervan, 1976.

Stibbs A.M. *1 Peter: A Commentary.* London, England: Tyndale Press, 1968: 77.

Thomas, W.H. Griffith, D.D. *Genesis: A Devotional Commentary.* Grand Rapids, Michigan: Eerdmans, 1946: 301. *(page 38)*

Scripture Index

Every effort has been made to include, nevertheless, every verse quoted or referred to. Scripture verses *are not always fully quoted within the text.*

Chapter 7: Joys and Trials
James 5:13
Psalm 37:3
Revelation 21:4
1 Timothy 1:16
James 1:2
1 Peter 1:6
John 8:44
2 Corinthians 12:7
John 13:27
Acts 2:23

Chapter 8: Heard
1 Samuel 1:1-20
James 5:13
Isaiah 53:4
1 Peter 5:7
Hebrews 11:1
Philippians 4:13
Romans 6:18,23
Psalm 46:1

Chapter 9: Why Pray - and How?
1 Samuel 1:1-20 (continued)
James 5:13
Deuteronomy 7:7,8
Romans 5:8
John 15:13
Ephesians 3:20 (KJV)
1 Samuel 1:3 (RSV)
1 Samuel 1:11 (NIrV)
Psalm 4:1
Matthew 9:27
Psalm 38:9
Romans 8:26
Matthew 6:6,9

Habakkuk 3:17,18
Psalm 16:11 (KJV)
Philippians 4:4

Chapter 10: A Discerning Heart
1 Kings 3:5-14
2 Chronicles 1:7-12
James 1:5
Ephesians 1:18
James 2:5
Romans 8:17
Matthew 6:19-21
Matthew 5:25-30 (RSV)
Matthew 5:25-33
Ephesians 3:16,20
Philippians 4:19
Colossians 2:2,3
John 3:16
Romans 6:23
Philippians 3:14
Colossians 3:23,24

Chapter 11: Ashamed and Disgraced
Ezra 9:6-15
Nehemiah 1:5-11
Romans 3:23
Isaiah 59:2
Exodus 20:3
Hosea 1:2
Micah 1:7,8
Judges 2:11,12,17,19
Judges 10:14,16
Lamentations 3:22
Romans 6:23a
1 John 1:9
Romans 10:9

Acts 3:19

Chapter 12: How Long?
Psalm 123:1-4
Habakkuk 1:2
Psalm 13:1,2
Psalm 40:1
Hosea 12:6b
Philippians 4:11,13
Hebrews 12:2
Colossians 3:2
Colossians 3:2
    (Jerusalem Bible)
Psalm 27:14
Psalm 37:7,34
Psalm 119:166
Psalm 130:5-7
Psalm 42:1
Psalm 63:1
Hebrews 11:10,13,14

Chapter 13: Focus
Psalm 25:1-22
Hebrews 12:2
Psalm 123:2b
Psalm 25:15-17
Isaiah 45:22 (KJV)

Chapter 14: Unfailing Love
Psalm 143
Romans 3:10,23
Romans 6:23
Philippians 4:19
Hebrews 4:16
1 Peter 5:8
Hebrews 2:14

1 John 3:8
Isaiah 53:10
Philippians 4:7
Matthew 9:38

Chapter 15: Saved from an Impossible Situation
Jonah 1-4
Luke 23:42,43
Psalm 40:2

Chapter 16: Power
Ephesians 1:17-23
Ephesians 3:14-19
2 Timothy 3:2-5
2 Corinthians 12:9, 10b
1 Samuel 17:38-40,45,46b,50
Ephesians 6:10
Matthew 6:1
Philippians 2:3,8
Ephesians 3:20

Chapter 17: God's Touch
Revelation 4:11
John 10:10
1 Timothy 6:17
Ephesians 3:19,20
Philippians 4:7
Psalm 16:11
1 Kings 19:11,12
1 Kings 19:12 (RSV)
Habakkuk 1:13

Chapter 18: Glory!
John 17:1-5, 20-26
Exodus 33:18,20,22
1 Timothy 6:16
John 1:14,18
John 12:23,28
John 19:28,30
Mathew 8:20
Luke 9:23
2 Corinthians 4:17
Psalm 16:11
Revelation 21:4

Seeking God's Face ©

Learning to Walk with God in Prayer

Book One
Paths of Peace Trilogy

Beryl Adamsbaum

10

Spring Will Come

When God Is Silent

"*I*sn't God supposed to make me happy?" asked Theresa, voicing a question which is perhaps at the back of many people's minds. Nowhere do the Scriptures imply that the Christian life is a bed of roses. Yes, the Bible talks of joy, peace, hope, and eternal life. All these are ours in Christ. But the Bible never hides the fact that Christians will suffer.

This book was initially going to be just a short series of devotional thoughts about prayer. Nothing complicated, nothing controversial. After all, we have many promises concerning answers to prayer in the Bible. "Call upon me in the day of trouble; I will deliver you," says God to his people (PSALM 50:15). "Ask and it will be given to you," says Jesus (MATTHEW 7:7). "Whatever you ask for in prayer, believe that you have received it, and it shall be yours" (MARK 11:24), to quote just three.

But what about the times when God is silent, when he doesn't seem to respond to our prayers? What do we make of verses in the Bible, like Job 13:24: "Why do you hide your face...?" or Psalm 74:1: "Why have you rejected us forever, O God?" And let us not forget that cry of anguish which escaped the lips of the Son of God himself, "My God, my God, why have you forsaken me?" (Matthew 27:46*b*)

જ⁊ જ⁊

We Feel Abandoned

Sometimes God seems far away. We cry out to him, but he does not seem to hear. We feel abandoned. "Lord, take away the pain!" we shout. But the ache is still there, the sick feeling in the pit of the stomach.

If you feel like that, you are definitely not alone, and you are in good company! The psalms are full of such expressions of despair.

My heart is in anguish within me;
the terrors of death assail me.
Fear and trembling have beset me;
horror has overwhelmed me (Psalm 55:4,5).

"I cried out to God for help;
I cried out to God to hear me.
When I was in distress, I sought the Lord;
at night I stretched out untiring hands
and my soul refused to be comforted....
Will the Lord reject forever?
Will he never show his favor again?
Has his unfailing love vanished forever?
Has his promise failed for all time?
Has God forgotten to be merciful?
Has he in anger withheld his compassion?
(Psalm 77:1,2,7,8,9)

How long, O Lord?
Will you hide yourself forever?

(Psalm 89:46*a*)

Hear my prayer, O Lord;
let my cry for help come to you.
Do not hide your face from me
when I am in distress.
Turn your ear to me;
when I call, answer me quickly.
(Psalm 102:1,2)

The psalmists pour out all their despairing feelings to God—their revolt, anguish, and distress. We need to do the same.

❧❧

Trusting God

Can we in all honesty ignore such cries from the heart? Can we skip over difficulties like these?

We may not have all the answers, but maybe we can at least give some thought to these problems. As we do, hopefully our eyes will be opened to discover a God who is far bigger than we had imagined, an infinite God who cannot be contained within the limits of human understanding, who cannot be boxed in, and who can show us the way!

"As the heavens are higher than the earth, so are my ways higher than your ways and my thoughts than your thoughts," says God (Isaiah 55:9). This almighty God came down to our level in the person of Jesus Christ, and he wants to have a relationship with us. He wants us to trust him. He wants us to pray to him, to seek his face. Because he is able!

What do we mean exactly when we talk about having faith? Do we mean that God will do everything we ask him to do and give us everything we want? Or do we mean that we submit to him and trust him to work out his purposes in accordance with his perfect will?

How do we feel and what do we think when God doesn't answer our prayers? We may have prayed for healing for someone who is sick, and that person has died. Did God not hear our prayers? Why did he not grant our request?

These are questions we cannot always answer. How can our finite minds possibly understand the ways of an infinite God? But let us not forget that this almighty God is also our heavenly Father, who loves us and wants the best for us.

Will we trust him? Difficulties can either draw us closer to God, as we wrestle with the problems, or cause us to harden our hearts in unbelief.

Do you sometimes feel, when you are wrestling in prayer, that you need to "pray a situation through," that is to say, pray on until God answers? Perhaps there are times when we need to do this. It was certainly the experience of Jacob, who told the Lord in no uncertain terms:

"I will not let you go until you bless me" (GENESIS 32:26).

At other times, we will just lay a disturbing problem before the Lord, as King Hezekiah did with a crucial letter:

"Hezekiah received the letter from the messengers and read it. Then he went up to the temple of the LORD and spread it out before the LORD" (2 KINGS 19:14). Having done that, we too will leave the matter with God and trust him to work in his way and in his time.

❧

The Unfolding of the Seasons

But how impatient we get sometimes! Why doesn't God provide instant answers? Sometimes he does, and we can praise him for that. Often he doesn't. Can we praise him then, too?

We want to see situations changed because of our prayers. We want to see lives transformed. It would seem that God's transforming work is usually progressive—a process, often long. Take the unfolding of the seasons, for example. It takes a long time for the sleep of winter to give way to the new life of spring, and even longer for the fruit on the trees to ripen and come to maturity.

God works in the same way in our lives and in the lives of those for whom we pray and the situations we bring before him. Winter seems very long and bleak at times. But spring will come!

God Will Never Forsake Us

When we are injured or incapacitated, we often feel alienated from God. We must not believe that feeling. God has promised that he will never abandon us: "Never will I leave you; never will I forsake you" (HEBREWS 13:5).

One thing we can always count on is his presence with us. When that terrible cry, "My God, my God, why have you forsaken me?" escaped the lips of Jesus, it was because he was bearing our sin—yours and mine—on the cross, so that never again would we be separated from our heavenly Father.

We read in Paul's letter to the Romans that nothing can separate us from God's love:

I am convinced that neither death nor life,
neither angels nor demons,
neither the present nor the future,
nor any powers,
neither height nor depth,
nor anything else in all creation,
will be able to separate us from the love of God
that is in Christ Jesus our Lord
(ROMANS 8:38,39).

ॐॐ

Purpose in Suffering

So many passages of Scripture deal with suffering in one way or another. We are exhorted to rejoice in our trials because we know that the outcome will be faith, refined and strengthened:

"Consider it pure joy, my brothers, whenever you face trials of many kinds, because you know that the testing of your faith develops perseverance," writes James (1:2,3).

The Apostle Peter adds: "You may have had to suffer grief in all kinds of trials. These have come so that your faith—of greater worth than gold, which perishes even though refined by fire —may be proved genuine and may result in praise, glory and honor when Jesus Christ is revealed" (1 Peter 1:6,7).

When we are called upon to suffer because of our faith, it means we share in the sufferings of Christ. For that reason, we can take heart, as Peter tells us. "Do not be surprised at the painful trial you are suffering.... But rejoice that you participate in the sufferings of Christ" (1 Peter 4:12,13).

We can also look beyond this world to that "eternal glory" which our present afflictions are achieving for us: "Our light and momentary troubles are achieving for us an eternal glory that far outweighs them all" (2 Corinthians 4:17).

Our troubles here and now, which may be severe and ongoing, are only qualified as "light and momentary" as they are compared and contrasted with the "eternal glory." Paul exclaims in his letter to the Romans: "I consider that our present sufferings are not worth comparing with the glory that will be revealed in us" (Romans 8:18).

Similarly, the writer of the letter to the Hebrews tells us that Jesus endured the pain and the shame of the cross for the "joy set before him" (Hebrews 12:2).

Knowing that there is a purpose in our suffering can give us the courage to go on. John White, in his book *The Cost of Commitment*, thanks God:

> ...that he can turn the suffering to serve his own purposes in my life. I thank him that because Jesus as man

suffered more than I ever will, God understands how I feel from personal experience. And as I praise and thank him, I become aware of two things. The suffering lessens. It lessens because the anxiety and fear that accompanied it have gone. (Peace in suffering halves its intensity.) In addition, hope is born as well as a sense of meaning in the suffering. I become almost excited that it will turn to my good. No longer do I wonder how I will bear the suffering. Suffering becomes a sort of chariot on which I ride to new planes of living.

And we will give the last word to the Apostle Paul, who writes: "To keep me from being conceited...there was given me a thorn in the flesh, a messenger of Satan, to torment me" (2 Corinthians 12:7).

Who gave him this "thorn"? He refers to it as a "messenger of Satan." Satan's purposes are always destructive: it was given in order to torment him.

And yet, Paul gives a positive reason too for this "thorn in the flesh." It was to prevent him from becoming conceited. (This may have been a special snare ahead of Paul, as we know that he was highly intelligent, among the most well-educated of his day and full of leadership abilities from God.) His suffering served, from Paul's perspective, a good, constructive purpose, originating surely in God. We can only conclude then that what Satan purposed for evil, God turned around and transformed into good.

❧❦

God's Grace Is Sufficient

God's answer to Paul's repeated prayer for deliverance from his suffering, before he reached acceptance of it, was, quite simply, "My grace is sufficient for you, for my power is made perfect in weakness" (2 CORINTHIANS 12:9).

If God's grace was sufficient for Paul, it is also sufficient for you today. His power is still "made perfect in weakness." Paul understood this, and it led him to utter that confident cry of victory and triumph: "I will boast all the more gladly about my weaknesses, so that Christ's power will rest on me. That is why, for Christ's sake, I delight in weaknesses, in insults, in hardships, in persecutions, in difficulties. For when I am weak, then I am strong" (2 CORINTHIANS 12:9,10).

This same strength is available to you in your weakness. Can you echo these triumphant, victorious, confident, glorious words of the Apostle Paul? Is this same experience yours? If not, it can be! ❧❦

Search me, O God, and know my heart...
PSALM 139:23

And we know that in all things God works for the good of those who love him, who have been called according to his purpose.

Romans 8:28

Opine
Publishing

Direct - Books - Order

Only Believe

— Learning to Walk with God in Trust

Book Two of the Prayer Trilogy — *Paths of Peace*

— Beryl Adamsbaum

Mail or Fax this order (pay by check or credit card):

Mail: Opine Publishing, P.O. Box 1239, Columbia, MD 21044 USA

✏ **Fax:** 410-730-0917

Number of Books:

_____ copies at $9.95 each $_____

USA Shipping & Handling (S/H): **FREE** U.S. SHIPPING

   INTERNATIONAL S/H: $3.95 (USD) $_____

   =========

                              TOTAL $_____

Method of Payment:

❑ Check, enclosed, **check #** _____

❑ Visa, MasterCard, AmEx *or* Discover ***Card #**_____

IF PAYING BY CREDIT CARD: *Name on Card _____

*Card Exp. (mm/yy)_____   *CARD CODE _____

Credit Card Billing Address: *Street/POB:_____

*City_____ *State _____ *Zip/Postal Code _____

Country (*if not USA) _____ *Tel. _____

* This information is required.

Ship to Address (If different from information above):

*Name_____

*Address_____

*City_____ *State_____ *Zip Code_____

Country (*if not U.S.A.) _____ (Tel. Codes) _____

E-mail Address_____ Tel. _____

* This information is required.

Mail Order Form and payment or card information to:

Opine Publishing, P.O. Box 1239, Columbia, Maryland (MD) 21044

Books for Life, Family, and Faith - **Thank you** *for your order!*

Opine
Publishing

Books for Life, Family, and Faith

Books for Life, Family, and Faith

Available from the Publisher and your favorite book-stores and online booksellers

Other books by Opine Publishing LLC:

Not All Roads Lead Home: A Story of Renewed Love
Jane Bullard
2004

Seeking God's Face: Learning to Walk with God in Prayer
Beryl Adamsbaum
2003

Exhausted Rapunzel: Tales of Modern Castle Life
Deirdre Reilly
2002

Opine Monograph:

Humanitarian & Government Issues
"The Perils of Unresolved Humanitarian Problems:
A Region of Crisis—the Middle East"
James N. Purcell, Jr.
2002

Coming Next…

PATHS OF PEACE

Learning to Walk with God Every Day

The third book of the
Paths of Peace Trilogy by
Beryl Adamsbaum

OPINE PUBLISHING - Books for Life, Family, and Faith

Available from Opine Publishing,
your local bookseller, and online

Opine
Publishing

Books for Life, Family, and Faith